The Most Misunderstood Women

"In *The Most Misunderstood Women of the Bible*, Mary DeMuth combines storytelling skills, love of Scripture, care for women, and her own personal experiences to create this riveting and intensely personal book. Using lovely imagery, Mary leads the reader into the biblical narrative in a way that allows these historically misunderstood ones to become flesh and blood women—your sister, your mother, your friend...you. Each chapter brought me to a place of reflection and meditation, offering rich insight, wisdom, and ultimately, hope."

—**Kay Warren**, co-founder, Saddleback Church

"Integrating creative storytelling with Bible commentary, Mary DeMuth invites readers to peer into the wounded hearts of women of Scripture who felt misunderstood and dismissed in their circumstances, and then skillfully guides readers through an exploration of their own experiences that parallel their biblical counterparts in pursuit of healing and a life of compassion and grace."

—**Missy Buchanan**, author of *From Dry Bones to Living Hope: Embracing God's Faithfulness in Late Life*

"Church tradition has often hidden the dramatic grace and restoration given freely to the women of Scripture. As Mary DeMuth lovingly shows, the God of the Bible relentlessly rewrites the legacies of those often considered failures, freely dispensing second glances and second chances to people whom those in power have pushed to the margins. Mary has done us a favor in recasting the story of these timeless women, pulling them from the shadows of judgment and into the sunlight of grace—reminding us of the same grace offered to each of us. Thanks for allowing me to be an early reader."

—**Steve Bezner**, pastor of Houston Northwest Church

"Filling these pages are a plaintive grief and a mournful empathy for the numerous women in the Bible who have been misunderstood, silenced, stereotyped, degraded, and mocked. Women who, like Hagar and Tamar and Bathsheba and Phoebe, have been brushed over in our Bible reading and preached as tropes of sin and shame. But Mary DeMuth, like a good old-fashioned Protestant, asks us to look again—at the text itself and the texture of the story, and she reveals to us women who deserve better because each was someone other than the trope taught us. I tried to pick my favorite revelation in *The Most Misunderstood Women of the Bible*, but I couldn't—I loved them all. Read this book with a renewal of empathy for stereotyped women."

> —**Scot McKnight,** professor of New Testament, Northern
> Seminary and author of *The Blue Parakeet, A Church
> called Tov* (with Laura Barringer)

"I've been misunderstood and it's a terrible feeling. Being misunderstood isn't lost on Jesus. He, too, was misunderstood, as were many women whose stories are shared in the Bible. If you've been wrongly accused or misunderstood, you're not alone. Mary DeMuth understands, and on the pages of this book she shows us how to learn from those who have gone before us so we can continue walking with our head held high. If you're human, you need this book."

> —**Jill Savage,** author of *Real Moms…Real Jesus* and host of
> the *No More Perfect Podcast*

"In *The Most Misunderstood Women of the Bible*, Mary writes in a compelling, creative, Christ-exalting way that causes you to reimagine stories in the Bible. You will be drawn deeper into the heart of God. Her skills as a world-class author and Bible teacher shine brightly. Men and women, buy this book for your-self and some friends. Study it. Marinate in it. Grow as a fol-lower of Jesus."

—**Dr. Derwin L. Gray,** co-founder and lead pastor of Trans-formation Church and author of *How to Heal The Racial Divide: What the Bible Says, and the First Christians Knew, about Racial Reconciliation*

"This is a sacred work. Mary DeMuth tenderly integrates heart and mind, scholarship and story, as she dignifies the narratives of women in the Bible whose reputations have long been misrep-resented and relegated to the status of taboo. Where others have picked up stones, DeMuth has covered these women with care-ful study, compelling imagination, and the compassion of God. Women will see both their pain and their hope in these pages. It is a compelling, artistic work of worship and faith."

—**Sharifa Stevens,** contributing author to *Vindicating the Vixens* and *Rally*

"There are few people I trust more than Mary DeMuth to handle women's stories with compassion, conviction, and great care. She has written a book that combines striking prose, beautifully dis-tilled truths, and poignant questions into one valuable resource for the church. These women's stories are a gift to the whole church, and uncovering them from under layers of misunderstanding and misogyny is a gift Mary has given us."

—**Kaitlyn Schiess,** author of *The Liturgy of Politics: Spiritual Formation for the Sake of Our Neighbor*

The Most Misunderstood Women of the Bible

The MOST MISUNDERSTOOD
WOMEN
of the BIBLE

What Their Stories Teach
Us About Thriving

MARY DeMUTH

SALEM
BOOKS
an imprint of Regnery Publishing
Washington, D.C.

Unless otherwise marked, all Scriptures are taken from the HOLY BIBLE, NEW LIVING TRANSLATION. Copyright © 1996, 2004, 2007 by Tyndale House Foundation. Used by permission of Tyndale House Publishers, Inc., Carol Stream, Illinois, 60188. All rights reserved.

Scripture quotations marked AMPC are taken from the Amplified® Bible. Copyright © 1954, 1958, 1962, 1964, 1965, 1987 by The Lockman Foundation. Used by permission. www.lockman.org

Scriptures marked CEV are taken from the CONTEMPORARY ENGLISH VERSION. Copyright © 1995 by the American Bible Society. Used by permission.

Scriptures marked ESV are taken from ESV® Bible (The Holy Bible, English Standard Version®), copyright © 2001 by Crossway, a publishing ministry of Good News Publishers. Used by permission. All rights reserved.

Scriptures marked GNT are taken from the Good News Translation® (Today's English Version, Second Edition). Copyright © 1992 American Bible Society. All rights reserved.

Scriptures marked HCSB are taken from the HOLMAN CHRISTIAN STANDARD BIBLE. Copyright © 1999, 2000, 2002, 2003 by Holman Bible Publishers in Nashville, Tennessee. All rights reserved.

Scriptures marked KJV are taken from the KING JAMES VERSION, public domain.

Scripture quotations marked MSG are taken from THE MESSAGE. Copyright © 1993, 1994, 1995, 1996, 2000, 2001, 2002. Used by permission of NavPress Publishing Group.

Scriptures marked NET are taken from the Bible® http://netbible.com copyright ©1996, 2019 used with permission from Biblical Studies Press, L.L.C. All rights reserved.

Scriptures marked WYC are taken from the Wycliffe Bible. Copyright © 2001 by Terence P. Noble.

Salem Books™ is a trademark of Salem Communications Holding Corporation
Regnery® is a registered trademark and its colophon is a trademark of Salem Communications Holding Corporation

ISBN: 978-1-68451-225-6
eISBN: 978-1-68451-289-8

Library of Congress Control Number: 2021946356

Published in the United States by
Salem Books
An Imprint of Regnery Publishing
A Division of Salem Media Group
Washington, D.C.
www.SalemBooks.com

Manufactured in the United States of America

10 9 8 7 6 5 4 3 2 1

*To Rebecca Carrell, Dr. Sandra Glahn, and Kelley Mathews:
Thank you for teaching me how to think biblically about the
brave women of the Bible. This book has your influence and
fingerprints all over it. I'm grateful for our lunches together.*

CONTENTS

Introduction

Over a decade ago, I shared with a friend about some angst I'd been experiencing after being misunderstood by a leader. I bled my woe-is-me sentences, feeling them glut my gut. "He assigned motives I don't even have," I said. "His assessment of me was not only unfair, but dead wrong."

She nodded, concern in her eyes.

I word-wrangled before her, trying to decide if I should approach the man and set him straight. I tallied important points, nearly spreadsheeting my rightness.

But then I stopped.

I took in a breath and finally said, "I don't think God has called me to reputation-management. I'm supposed to trust Him in the midst of being misunderstood."

That's when the seed of this book dropped into my heart. She looked at me, then asked, "Did you know Jesus was the most misunderstood person to walk the earth?"

I said nothing.

In that place of quiet, my mind frantically retraced the life of Jesus: teaching in the Temple at twelve as his parents panicked, then getting reprimanded by them. Questioning the religious elite who held the supposed keys to the Kingdom (though He was King of it all). Praising despised outcasts, while making insider Pharisees the villains in parables. Speaking to a Samaritan woman at the well, as his bewildered disciples looked on. And yet, Jesus received people's blatant misunderstanding and usually said nothing. He endured it. He ventured into the mountains to tell His Father about it. And then He dusted off His sandals (and heart) and took the next Kingdom step. He fulfilled his mission despite all that questioning. And because He did, we can, too.

My friend's question illuminated a truth new to me: Jesus understands being misunderstood. And since He has endured misunderstanding, empathy abounds for those of us walking the same path. There's a little piece of encouraging advice in Hebrews 12, tucked in after the author speaks of Jesus enduring the torturous cross. "Think of all the hostility he endured from sinful people; then you won't become weary and give up" (Hebrews 12:3).

I'm now at that place in my life where grand lessons take shape in my mind, and this is one: being misunderstood is one of the hardest things we humans endure this side of eternity. Even so, we don't have to live sidelined, crafting reputation-defending spreadsheets until we die. There is a more hopeful, vibrant way.

Though my friend shared an important truth about Jesus, the biblical narrative also presents the stories of many who have endured the hardship of misunderstanding. Perhaps this is felt even more keenly in the stories of the women of the Bible—stories we don't grow up hearing, those of women whose real lives are seldom depicted. Or, if they are represented in faded flannel-graphs, they are often maligned or dismissed.

Eve bears the wrath of the entire human race.

Hagar is relegated to second-tier significance.

Leah's weak-eyed heartache is dismissed rather than explored.

Rahab is remembered as Rahab the harlot, diminishing her audacious faith.

Naomi, the bitter one in the book of Ruth, becomes a depressed flashback.

Bathsheba has been preached about as a seductress, seldom taking into account the dynamics of power and kingship.

Tamar's horrific story of rape in 2 Samuel 13 is rushed through or never highlighted.

The Proverbs 31 woman has been retrofitted to fit various cultural norms without dealing honestly with the text or the context in which her chapter is written.

Mary of Magdala is often referred to (incorrectly) as a former prostitute.

And Phoebe, who many scholars believe carried the book of Romans to Rome, is a historical afterthought.

These are merely a handful of the women in the Bible who suffer under the weight of misunderstanding. And they have much to teach all of us—about grit, tenacity, endurance, and hope. They will be our tutors as we mine the idea and reality of being misunderstood.

I'm going to present each woman as someone real (because that is the truth). So often we read the Scriptures as if the stories therein were full of cardboard archetypes who occupy a blip of time and nothing more. But these women? They *lived*. Like us, they harbored painful secrets, melted under the weight of stress, and broke in the same places we break today. They walked through the mundane rituals of daily life, asked for advice when bewildered, and wondered at their significance. They bled, hurt for others, and faced pestilence, uncertainty, and death. They are us. We are them.

I will don my fiction hat and flesh each woman out for you. I will portray her story, closely aligned with Scripture and scholarship, but in a way that empowers you to really see her, perhaps for the first time.

After her narrative, I'll explore how she navigated the misunderstanding seas, highlighting other parts of Scripture that enlighten us toward inner understanding and positive praxis—the practical working out of our salvation. While this book will give you new insight, it's not for your head only—it's for your heart, then your feet. As Paul reminds us in Philippians 2:12, "Therefore, my dear friends, as you have always obeyed—not only in my presence, but now much more in my absence—continue to work out your salvation with fear and trembling." I believe we can grow in our understanding of misunderstanding and, through that learning process, begin to act as Jesus did—with perseverance. You no longer need to be swayed by the opinion of others. Even if friends or family members malign you, or strangers on social media threaten to expose you according to their prejudice, you can keep walking forward, thanks to the powerful lessons you will learn in the pages of this book.

My sincere prayer is that you'll be refreshed and invigorated to face each day with expectation, despite the cacophony of maligning voices our culture seems to coddle. Because your misunderstood-ness, though it feels very real, does not define your worth. The Misunderstood One does.

CHAPTER ONE

Eve, the Blamed One

Her name sounded like the intake of a breath, followed by a worried exhale. *Ha-vah*. In and out, Eve's breath steadied under a brilliant sky. Adam had given her that name—to breathe, to give life—after the darkest day, the day of nakedness, self-knowing, and judgment. It was Yahweh's stunning gift—this life—after her decision resulted in death. If only she could retract the movement of her arm reaching treeward, mesmerized by the promise of knowledge. But some things remained unfixable.

Now Adam and Eve possessed language that beheld time—Before, After.

Before became halcyon. Trees bore juice-laden fruit. The ground yielded its produce in easy surrender. The animals shook paws in friendship. No death. No decay. No shame. Not a bit of flesh. Just life, and life abundant.

In the dawn of Eden, the great Garden, she had borne no name. As Adam busied himself in taxonomy, placing creatures into categories, the Lord approached him (at least this is how he relayed it to her later) and placed him under languid sleep. In the helplessness of slumber, the Lord removed bone from ribcage, fashioning a companion, an *ezer kenegdo*. Her—one who was strong to his weakness, a come-alongside rescuer. The two words would later refer to God, the One who always had a secret rescue mission even when all seemed lost. But Adam, bewildered by this creature before him, gave her no name. Instead, he categorized her. "Woman," he called her. *Ishah* because she was taken from *ish*, man. She corresponded to him, fit his embrace.

Before.

They'd adventure in the cool of the day among the creatures, gathering food at will, rejoicing in each other's conversation. They learned the intricacies of the other's delights as they walked alongside the Lord, who Himself modeled self-giving love. Know the other. Find out what brings a smile. Keep delighting. Give, give, give.

The hiss in the creature's lilting speech haunted her nightmares in the After. Seductive. Wise beyond his serpentine years. Clever. Logical. He, too, wanted to walk in the Garden as the Lord did—and he did so with cloying curiosity, as if on mission.

She found herself near the forbidden tree when he sidled up to her, though Adam stood nigh. The tree piqued her curiosity simply because Adam had relayed its forbiddenness to her one afternoon soon after she first opened her eyes in Eden. There the tree stood now, stately, arms reaching heavenward, roots grappling earth. It loomed above all the other trees in curious majesty as the doves sang love songs in its branches. She breathed it all in, then exhaled.

"Did God really say you must not eat the fruit from any of the trees in the garden?" the serpent asked, smiling.

The question pushed her off-kilter. *What? Did God say what?* She remembered Adam's words—no, all trees were lawful, only one bore the awful prohibition.

She looked at Adam, but he gave no answer. Though he stood next to her, he seemed strangely distant.

"Of course we may eat fruit from the trees in the garden." She scanned the trees dotting the green hills and vales. She pointed to *the* tree, its fruit ruby red under the azure sky. "It's only the fruit from the tree in the middle of the garden that we are not allowed to eat." As she spoke, a breeze rustled through its branches, causing the fruit to dance—enchanting her eyes. She found her voice. "God said, 'You must not eat it or even touch it; if you do, you will die.' That's what Adam instructed. Right, Adam?"

Adam remained mute, and his eyes registered neither worry nor concern. As placid as a lake in morning.

Eve understood nothing of death in the Before. She had no frame of reference for the term. It certainly sounded foreboding, particularly at night when her mind fixated on the word: *death*. But wasn't God the author of all life? Who was He, really? Wasn't He their kindhearted companion, full of energy and power and compassion? Hadn't He indicated that He wanted the very best for them?

The serpent rose to her eye level and laughed. "You won't die!"

The wind stopped. The tree stood perfectly still. The air felt rigid, unfamiliar. The lie tasted sweet, or at least that's how she remembered the serpent's sentence in the After.

"God knows that your eyes will be opened as soon as you eat it, and you will be like God, knowing both good and evil."

The Lord is a miser, she thought. *He is withholding something from me that would make me wise. Is He good? Or is He selfish, keeping all that wisdom and power to Himself?* In the sorry wisdom she gained in the After, these became the musings of a madwoman.

With a fierce longing for more, she looked up at the tree. Its fruit's scent wafted before her—a mixture of roses, eucalyptus, and lemon blossoms. If one could drink its perfume, she would. In that moment, all the woman wanted was the fruit scented like Heaven—the very thing the Lord selfishly withheld from her.

She asked herself again, *Is God good?* Why would a good God forbid such a tantalizing fruit? What was He holding back from her, from Adam? He had always seemed forthcoming and kind—powerful, too. But did that façade hold a secret? And would that secret make her understand her world better? Though the Garden held fascination, it boasted complexities as well. Perhaps this wisdom tree could grant her deeper knowledge—of how things grew, of how best to shepherd the animals in her care. All this tending of flora and fauna became tedious.

A sunbeam highlighted a single globed fruit. She approached it. Drank in its intoxicating scent. Looked back at Adam—who still uttered not one word. What could one bite hurt? Her stomach rumbled. In one fluid, horrid motion, she grasped the rounded fruit with its red, supple skin and took a bite. The flesh dripped blood-red from her lips, and before she could register its taste, she handed the bitten fruit to Adam, who bit large.

In looking back at Before, she remembered the fruit's shape-shifting taste, from heady and sweet to bitter as bile. She wanted to expel it from her body, but the poison had already invaded her mind. A deep sadness permeated her. The first prick of dread, too—the birth of regret turning pregnant with shame. She glanced down at her torso, once a body she thought nothing about, and suddenly realized her nakedness. Her breath came in sips as she and Adam gathered leaves to cover their bodies while the serpent laughed maniacally.

The rest of the day was spent in tedious covering, fashioning fashion with leaves of fig trees. Though both thought a quick sewing job would undo their fateful decision, vulnerability and panic roared to life. Superficial remedies would not work for such a gaping wound. Fear gripped them both, snaking through their once-sweet relationship. Adam spat suspicions Eve's way. She spat them right back.

But as dusk fell upon Eden, Eve's stomach lurched. The Lord would appear, and they would have to face Him. Where was the serpent now that the Lord's fragrance wafted through the underbrush? He had slithered away, his job finished.

Adam pulled Woman into the tree line, indicating they needed to hide.

Three words wafted through the Garden.

Where...

are...

you?

Adam stepped out from their limbed hiding place, covered in leaves. "I heard you walking in the garden, so I hid. I was afraid because I was naked," he said, no longer muted.

It was then she noticed the Lord's broken gaze—disappointment, holy anger, grief, exasperation...and yet? Settledness.

"Who told you that you were naked?" the Lord God asked Adam.

Why had he not addressed her first? Hadn't she ruined everything? Why did God direct his accusation toward Adam, the man of few words?

The Lord God continued, "Have you eaten from the tree whose fruit I commanded you not to eat?" Again, directed toward Adam.

She remembered her husband's silence, how he left the decision solely to her. How vulnerable she had felt under the serpent's stare. An apology practically burst from her chest before the Almighty questioned her, but Adam's words came first.

"It was the woman You gave me who gave me the fruit, and I ate it."

Is this what knowing good and evil means? Blame? Betrayal? Being categorized through taxonomy? But inside her slithered a deeper worry: utter unworthiness. In Before, the earth felt solid beneath her feet. She knew her place, felt it like gold weighting her bones. Her feet stood on the rock of being valued, wanted, loved. But with the first taste of the fruit, suspicion crept in, causing her to doubt the Lord

God's goodness and her husband's once-kindhearted affection. Now, as Adam's words of blame sank into her, the earth felt quivery beneath her, and her equilibrium shifted toward chaos.

The Lord God looked into Eve's eyes, which now held the world's cares in creviced lines. His sadness she could not bear. She looked away, swallowed bile. Choked on her tears.

"What have you done?" He asked.

At first, she said nothing. She looked to her closest companion, her confidant, but Adam met her eyes with a sneer. She exhaled sorrow. She wanted to say she was sorry, but those words felt so insignificant. Perhaps if she could reason with the Lord God, let Him know how she had been tricked. "Serpent deceived me," she said. "That's why I ate it."

And as she uttered the word *serpent*, he slithered back, a victory living behind a cold gaze. He pulled himself to full height, but even so, the Lord God dwarfed him both in stature and goodness.

With holy anger, the Lord God said, "Because you have done this, you are cursed more than all animals, domestic and wild. You will crawl on your belly, groveling in the dust as long as you live." With those words, the serpent melted from tall stature to dust. He would rise to his feet no more.

The Lord God looked at Eve. "And I will cause hostility between you and the woman, and between your offspring and her offspring. He will strike your head, and you will strike his heel."

In the After, she pondered these declarations many times, rolling them through her thoughts, but she could not make sense of them.

As dusk turned to night, the Lord God said, "I will sharpen the pain of your pregnancy, and in pain you will give birth. And you will desire to control your husband, but he will rule over you."

Again, she would think on these words during her sojourn on Earth. When she first heard them, she didn't understand she would experience what the creatures of the Garden had—pregnancy and birth. None of them whimpered through the experience, but she would howl and pant when her time arrived. The conviviality between her and Adam had been irrevocably removed. No longer side-by-side companions, they battled each other, but because of his sinewy strength, he would always win. The serpent sewed truth and lies together when he whispered his empty promises. She *did* know good and evil, but she now experienced the working out of evil in her, in Adam. All this so-called wisdom brought was loneliness.

The Lord God turned to Adam and said, "Since you listened to your wife and ate from the tree whose fruit I commanded you not to eat, the ground is cursed because of you."

She heard Adam groan then. Their blessed ground cursed; what would that mean? As when the serpent stood by, Adam said nothing.

"All your life, you will struggle to scratch a living from it," the Lord God continued. "It will grow thorns and thistles for you, though you will eat of its grains. By the sweat of your brow will you have food to eat until you return to the ground from which you were made. For you were made from dust, and to dust you will return."

She kicked at the soil, then. It had been rich, black humus prior to her bite, but now? Waterless dust kicked into the air. She coughed.

All felt lost.

Until Adam spoke.

"Eve," he said to the dusted wind. "Your name is Eve, the mother of all who live." *Ha-vah.*

On the darkest day of history, when death and curses reigned tantamount, Adam laced his voice with hope. Adam and Eve would live first before they tasted death. Life would persevere, though never as abundant—and it would have an end point. Under the canopy of stars, now dimmed substantially from the night prior, the Lord God took the life of an animal, its blood running onto the thirsty earth. Now, Eve, the mother of all who lived, smelled death's stench for the first time. Bloodshed tainted everything in the After, she knew.

And yet, from the sacrifice of one animal, the Lord God covered them in its skin—yet another symbol of grace in chaos.

The Lord God lifted His hands skyward and spoke as the earth quaked beneath His voice. "Look," He said. "The human beings have become like Us, knowing both good and evil. What if they reach out, take fruit from the tree of life, and eat it? Then they will live forever!"

He banished Adam and Eve from the Garden of Eden. Adam, made from earth, would have to conquer its brambles. The Lord God stationed mighty cherubim to the east of the Garden and placed in their hands flaming swords that flashed back and forth to defend the way to the Tree of Life.

Thus began the ever After, the undulating monotony of tilling and conflict. She began as Woman, then ended as Eve. But between the nomenclatures, the greatest tragedy of humankind loomed as tall as the Tree of the Knowledge of Good and Evil, now locked away behind flaming swords.

In the days after banishment, Eve found solace in the arms of Adam. Though his hands roughened from toiling in the soil, she welcomed his embrace. The bile she'd experienced from the tree's fruit returned, but this time she could expel her stomached food. For months this happened as her belly grew outward—a wondrous thing. She remembered the female animals with their swollen bellies prior to birthing, and she thanked God for the gift of life. Though she had made a fatal choice, God granted her the kick of a child within her womb. On the day of completion, she screamed her pain, but as Cain rushed to the world into the hands of a bewildered Adam-as-midwife, Eve could not help but exclaim, "With the LORD's help, I have produced a man!"

They named him Cain because he had been acquired—like a gift from God.

But Eve had no tutor to teach her the ways of motherhood. She, born of Adam's side, had no mother, had never suckled at the breast.

Everything Cain presented to her was a new conundrum, a fearful gift. When would he roll from side to side? How could she corral him when he crawled in the dust? How long should she allow him to drink from her breast? And when would he stand erect? Every new development filled Eve with wonder and dread. What a privilege it was to be like the Lord God, shepherding a human being, but what a responsibility, too. She had to learn every aspect of motherhood from the animals, but she found that Cain's dependence upon her lasted much longer than a lioness's cubs. She would be his guardian for years, not months. When something perplexed her beyond her abilities, she would ask Adam, and if they both bent under the weight of parental confusion, they walked with the Lord God and asked for His help.

Soon after the arrival of Cain, Eve's stomach reacted as her belly extended once again. Abel, the boy whose name meant "fleeting breath," cried his way into the world—and as he did, Cain's jealous animosity toward him grew.

Cain—the son of his father—had a heart that was stitched to the land, and everything he touched flourished surprisingly under his cultivation. The first crops he devoured, hungry for the affirmation of achievement they brought, a trophy to his abilities. After the first fruits died back into the earth, Cain gathered a few bits and pieces left over and presented them to the Lord God as an afterthought. And then, as all farmers after him would, he turned his attention to the next season.

Abel loved the animals in his care. He whispered life over his lambs as the wind rustled the leaves above. While sheep bleated in chorus, Abel's response was praise: he brought the very best of the sheepfold to give to the Lord God in offering. Eve noticed this dedication, and she encouraged Abel's fidelity to their God.

But she also noticed the darkened stares of Cain, particularly after God rejected his offering and accepted Abel's. The Lord God had warned Cain of impending doom if he didn't master his anger, but

Cain responded by pouring wrath into his countenance. It soured his heart, Eve knew, so she did her best to protect Abel from Cain's wrath.

But you cannot protect everyone all the time, she soon learned.

One day the brothers left for the fields together, but Cain returned alone.

The Lord, in the dusk of day, approached Cain. "Where is your brother? Where is Abel?" Eve could not help but remember the echo of God's first question to them after their taste of forbidden fruit. *Where are you?*

"I don't know," Cain responded. "Am I my brother's guardian?"

But the Lord said, "What have you done?"—the same four words He had asked Eve in the Garden. Her mouth had dripped red then, and now Cain's hands were wet with crimson under a too-hot sun. He could not scrub the blood free, so he remained silent—like father, like son.

Eve felt Abel's expiration in her lungs. She who breathed in and out as the mother of all the living, exhaled dread. The boy named "fleeting breath" no longer inhaled life. Now Eve fully understood the curse of death, knowing good and evil. The tree's fruit brought no vitality—it only ushered in heartache, the kind that cries after the womb, then rips away her child from the land of the living. She was now wise in the ways of grief. *What do you do when you run out of tears?*

"Listen!" God said. At that moment, a lion's ferocious roar reverberated through the day, shaking the earth. "Your brother's blood cries out to me from the ground!" The Lord God cursed Cain's relationship with the earth even more than he had cursed Adam's—a burden too great to bear. In mercy, the Lord God marked Cain's flesh—a moniker of warning to anyone who harmed him. Cain migrated away from Eve's realm, leaving her alone with Adam, bereft and barren.

But even in death and tragedy, life sprang again. A third son graced Eve's life, and she named him "appointed one"— Seth. It was in Seth's children that the reversal happened: just as Eve and Adam had called on the Lord God by name in the Garden of Eden, Seth's children worshipped Him by name.

Eve died east of Eden, but life continued still.

The Biblical Narrative

Each time you read the first few chapters of the book of Genesis, you'll discover nuances and insights. This last time through, I began to see parallels between Adam and Cain. God asked both similar questions: *Where are you? Where is your brother?* And he cursed the ground in the aftermath of each of their sins. Like father, like son.

But what of Eve? What can we learn about her as we mine the treasures of Scripture?

First, you may have noticed that Eve was first called Woman by Adam, and then after the Fall, he named her Eve. This naming on both sides of the narrative is called an *inclusio*, "a repetition of two ideas that bookend a discourse. Inclusios serve as valuable signposts. They signal an important point in the text."[1] The whole pristine world fell apart in the middle of the two namings—a problem God would remedy through the sending of His Son.

In Genesis 2:23 after God had fashioned the woman, Adam exclaimed, "At last! This one is bone from my bone, and flesh from my flesh! She will be called 'woman,' because she was taken from 'man.'" In verse 24, we learn about the covenant of marriage, where a man leaves his family of origin and becomes a new family, united as one with his wife. The chapter ends with, "Now the man and his wife were both naked, but they felt no shame" (2:25).

The story begins with Adam classifying the animals, then classifying his wife in a similar manner. Notice when the serpent approaches her, he calls her "Woman," not "Eve," because she has yet to be named. But after the Fall, Adam gives her a personal name, "Eve," which hints at life and hope. In the middle of the story of deception and eating the forbidden fruit, the shame that had been utterly absent now invaded both husband and wife, causing them to hide and try to cover themselves. Woman, no shame, deception and sin, shame, Eve. Inclusio.

Scripture blames Adam for the Fall, though there is no doubt he shared responsibility with the serpent and Eve. "Just as everyone dies because we all belong to Adam, everyone who belongs to Christ will be given new life" (1 Corinthians 15:22). It's common, however, for people to solely blame Eve for the fall of humankind. But read the text again.

God confronted Adam first. And throughout the New Testament, we see blame leveled at him, not his wife. "Because one person [Adam] disobeyed God, many became sinners. But because one other person [Jesus] obeyed God, many will be made righteous" (Romans 5:19).

Not only that, but Eve honestly confessed what she did and placed blame on an appropriate villain. Satan deceived her; she ate. But when Adam is confronted, he not only blames Eve, he also makes God a villain: "It was the woman *You* gave me" (emphasis mine). While Eve did not question God or assign blame to Him, Adam instead chose a twofold blame game. Eve handed him the forbidden fruit, yes, but it was God's fault for creating the very woman he had once declared joy over. Bone of his bone, flesh of his flesh, in light of the Fall, has now become a liability—a terrible gift from a God who harmed Adam in the giving of it. Eve blamed evil personified. Adam blamed God.

We forget that both were present in the eating. We overlook that Adam stood there as the Serpent hissed lies, never countering his slander of God. Humanity's fall into sin was a two-sexed failure, but Eve often gets blamed.

How This Applies to Misunderstood You

When I considered adding Eve to the narrative of this book, I knew that many, many people had misunderstood her, placing upon her shoulders the sole blame for humanity's problem with sin. But what about in her context? Had she been misunderstood in the Garden as well? And how does that apply to us today?

Adam, when asked about what he and his wife had lost beneath the Tree of the Knowledge of Good and Evil, did not admit his own culpability, as I mentioned before. He did not confess his sin with contrition and holy fear. Instead, he projected blame, attributing malevolence to Eve, then God. She and she alone was at fault for eating the fruit, though its juices still dripped from his chin. The truth was they both were to blame. Both participated in the deed, and both would carry consequences. Deflecting blame, then, is as old as the Garden, but that doesn't make it easier to bear.

What do you do when someone shifts blame entirely on you? How do you feel when you are the scapegoat of someone else's continued problems? We see this in divorce situations, where blame typically falls on both sides, yet one spouse attributes the entirety of the aftermath to one person. They draw sides, convincing others of their story, and because that story is the first thing a confidant hears, the hearer is quick to believe it, proving Proverbs 18:17 true. "The first to speak in court sounds right—until the cross-examination begins."

One thing I've learned during my years of following Christ is this: we are not called to micromanage our reputations when we're maligned. We speak the truth, yes, but we need not entangle ourselves in the unfair narratives of another. And before we react to someone's seemingly unfair blame, we have to go back to Jesus and examine ourselves. Once, when I felt led to talk to a friend about her gossiping habit, I realized that I was a hypocrite. I had gossiped too. I got on my knees, asked God to search me and reveal my own sins, and only after a lot of repentance, reading the Bible, and consulting with a mature believer did I venture forward in talking to my friend. Even so, she misunderstood my intent and backed away.

Seldom do we see a clean-cut version of what Matthew 18:15–17 describes when we confront someone with their sin.

> If another believer sins against you, go privately and point out the offense. If the other person listens and confesses it, you have won that person back. But if you are unsuccessful, take one or two others with you and go back again, so that everything you say may be confirmed by two or three witnesses. If the person still refuses to listen, take your case to the church. Then if he or she won't accept the church's decision, treat that person as a pagan or a corrupt tax collector.

Confrontation moves from small to big, one-on-one to a crowd, but so often in today's world, we do the opposite. Instead of working out a misunderstanding one to the other, we start with social media, convincing others of our rightness. When we begin with the crowd, we are in danger of the sin of self-righteousness, and in that place, our heart hardens, bitterness comes, and we end up closing off the pathway to reconciliation.

Like we are apt to do, Adam started globally with his blame. God's fault. Eve's fault. He did not start with himself. Nor did he pull Eve aside quietly and work through their sin together. His first intent was to lash out publicly, shifting blame from himself to another.

Blame-shifting is as old as the Garden, but that does not lessen its bite in our lives.

Another misunderstanding I see in the narrative is a bit nuanced. While Adam shifted the blame, Eve misunderstood the good intentions of her good God. While she entertained the voice of the serpent, her mind clouded. Though she had a history of experiencing God's kindness in the Garden and had no reason to doubt His benevolence, once Satan introduced doubt in the form of a question, she allowed that mystery to needle her understanding of what she knew to be true. In the Before,

God could be trusted. He cared for the first family well. He provided nourishment, light, and peace. But in the fulcrum between Before and After, doubt sprouted. Eve's single-minded devotion to God wavered. She disbelieved His care, so she took her care into her own hands. Her newfound worry caused her to do just what Oswald Chambers warns against: "All our fret and worry is caused by calculating without God."[2]

Misunderstanding God and His goodness births all sorts of heartache. When we let fear reign, we are far more vulnerable to sin, and we lose sight of the great mission God has for us. The Apostle Paul mentioned this caution when he wrote, "But I fear that somehow your pure and undivided devotion to Christ will be corrupted, just as Eve was deceived by the cunning ways of the serpent" (2 Corinthians 11:3). To give into deception is to misunderstand God and to forgo our important Kingdom mission: to live devoted, undivided lives.

We must guard our minds because deception and lies are the language of the world we live in. When Jesus rebuked the Pharisees, He compared them to the devil: "For you are the children of your father the devil, and you love to do the evil things he does. He was a murderer from the beginning. He has always hated the truth, because there is no truth in him. When he lies, it is consistent with his character; for he is a liar and the father of lies" (John 8:44).

Satan will do everything he can to make us misunderstand the good intentions of our Father. When we doubt God's benevolence, we become prone to reaching for our own solutions. This is why Paul offers a stern warning to us: misunderstanding God's character leads to sin. "And it was not Adam who was deceived by Satan. The woman was deceived, and sin was the result" (1 Timothy 2:14).

Even when all seemed lost, even after fruit dripped red from her mouth and the world darkened irreparably, grace came. Woman became *Ha-vah*, the one who breathed, the embodiment of life. It's the same for you. When people unfairly shift blame to you, you can choose to praise God for the breath in your lungs. In this broken world, He continues to sustain you. When you misunderstand the good intentions of God and take a bite of sin, you are graced with forgiveness through the life, death, and resurrection of Jesus, who called Himself "the life" (see John 14:6). Whether misunderstood or misunderstanding, life still can flourish in the aftermath. Though the enemy's intention against you meant harm and death, his winter cannot last; spring must burst forth. We see the truth of the Gospel in John 10:10: "The thief's purpose is to steal and kill and destroy. My purpose is to give them a rich and satisfying life."

Eve experienced life after the Fall. She bore children, mourned the loss of her son, and continued to work the land. The Bible doesn't reveal how long she lived or how she died, which in itself is its own testimony. That she lived beyond her bite of forbidden fruit reveals the outlandish *hesed* (loyal, covenantal love) of God. That same God holds you, even when you distance yourself from Him through sin. He pursues you, loves you, and bears the weight of your sin. He understands what it's like to be a scapegoat for someone else's sin. "For God made Christ, who never sinned, to be the offering for our sin, so that we could be made right with God through Christ" (2 Corinthians 5:21). We may live under the shadow of Adam and Eve's original sin, but because of Jesus, we can be forgiven and receive new life. This is good news, and we can rest in it.

Truths about Fully Understood You

- Though you make mistakes, God's grace is greater.
- Even when you are blamed (or genuinely at fault), you always have the choice to do the next right thing.
- There is life after your heartache.
- Because of the Spirit within you, you can discern and overcome deception.

Questions for Discussion

1. What surprised you about Eve's story? In what ways have you misunderstood her up until now?

2. How does knowing Adam was present at the temptation change the way you read the biblical text?

3. What lies have you believed over the past year? How have you discerned that they actually were lies? Have you retrained your mind to believe the truth, and if so, how have you done that?

4. No one is all good (except Jesus) or all bad. Here we see a complicated origin story of sin and grace. How does knowing our fragility help you better understand God's grace?

5. How did God demonstrate grace to Eve? How does He demonstrate grace to you?

CHAPTER TWO

Hagar, the Forgotten One

Hagar had no time to prepare her heart for what the day would bring, but she should have known that life would kidnap her again. She whose name meant "flight" flew without joy from the blessings of the Nile into enslavement to a wealthy family far from her homeland. All she knew was loss—but she especially grieved her Egyptian family. Was her mother still alive? Her father, long sleeping with the gods, left so little behind that Mother had no choice but to take her girl and sell her in order to ensure her own survival. Hagar could not remember Mother's jasmine scent, though she sometimes could still hear the lilt of her song wafting through her dreams. She would reach her arms toward the melody, but Mother always disappeared in a mist. Her dream presence had been a happy oasis, but as she misted away, only the desert of Canaan remained.

It was another such dusty day in the plains when Sarai overturned Hagar's will. Though she toiled under the scrutiny of a lamenting mistress, Hagar kept to herself, reimagining life outside their compound.

But Sarai would not stop talking. Words like "barren," "empty," and "childless" punctuated her speech until one day it reached a siren pitch.

Sarai gripped Hagar's forearm with new strength and pulled her into the dusty encampment near Abram's tent. Sarai let go. Hagar turned to leave, thinking this was merely another of her grieving rants, but Sarai told her to stay—with no words but a stern look that anchored Hagar to the dust beneath her feet.

Abram exited his tent, nodding to Sarai. He asked how she was doing, and then settled his gaze upon her in anticipation of the torrent of words that would soon fly his way.

"The Lord has prevented me from having children," Sarai said.

But what of the promise? Hagar wondered. Their God had covenanted a promise of a son in the future. The whole camp knew the story of the smoking firepot and the flaming torch, where Yahweh had punctuated His promise with fire. Surely Sarai remembered the promise of offspring!

Sarai gripped Hagar's forearm again, pulling her toward Abram. "Go and sleep with my servant," she said. "Perhaps I can have children through her."

A slave has no say in these matters, but Hagar suddenly wished she could sprout wings and fly back to Egypt. Though she knew it to be foolish, she had allowed herself to dream of freedom, marriage, and motherhood—but this way? All those dreams felt cruel now, ridiculous even. Sarai's words burned her ears, incinerating hope. She could say nothing, but wished her internal words would reach Abram: *No, wait for the promise through your wife. Not me. Not now. Do not do this.*

Hagar slipped into shock as she felt Sarai push her into the darkness of Abram's tent. This was no marriage, no home, no dream.

But Abram, beaten down from the extended wait for a son, agreed. He reasoned that perhaps God had never meant him to have a child with

Sarai, but some other way. His ways, it had been said, were mysterious, after all. Would having Abram's child set Hagar free from this slavery? Would life change for the better? She wanted to hope, but dared not.

Later, something rose up in Hagar when she felt the knowing of women, the illness of morning, the distension of her womb. It was a fierce, loyal longing for her child—someone of her own to love. Sarai, who had never known motherhood, who had pushed Hagar into Abram's arms, now was diminished in Hagar's sight. This tiny bit of power morphed into mockery. She could conceive, but Sarai could not. Her words came out cutting.

She watched as Sarai threw her arms toward the desert sky. Gesturing toward Hagar, Sarai told Abram, "This is all your fault! I put my servant into your arms, but now that she's pregnant she treats me with contempt. The LORD will show you who's wrong—you or me!"

Abram hung his head, then shook it slowly from side to side. He put his hand tenderly on Sarai's cheek. "Look," he said. "She is your servant, so deal with her as you see fit." In that hiccup of words, Hagar's mockery shuddered to meekness under Sarai's treatment. The wife of Abram scourged her with disdainful words, made fun of her, and excluded her from the best food in the camp. Hagar swallowed moldy bread, praying the morsel wouldn't harm her growing child. The abuse Hagar had heaped on Sarai now boomeranged back upon her in a torrent, and she regretted what she had started. The wrath of the childless woman could be tasted throughout the camp.

Hagar took Sarai's words without retaliating. Endured the harsh treatment. Slept minimally with one eye open. Feared for her life. All this she did for the baby kicking within her, so the infant could have a home and be safe as the child of Abram. She forgot her life, forgot her longings, forgot Egypt, until her focus became a pinhole of concentration. She would persevere—not for herself, but for this child.

One day Sarai's mockery hinted at violence, and in that moment, the dam of fear released through Hagar. She feared for her child's life.

Without packing or hesitation, she scurried away from their encampment in the hollow of night toward freedom from the tyranny of a slaveowner's wife. Wild animals and starvation seemed easier to endure than the cold, angry stare of a Sheol-bent woman.

No longer able to call Kadesh "home," Hagar hoped to make her way to Bered. Initially, she fueled her flight with the agitated frenzy of fear, but as she progressed along the road to Shur and came upon unfamiliar trees on the outskirts of the wilderness, she questioned her escape. Legs swollen from too much trekking, eyes droopy from exhaustion, Hagar sat beside a spring of water. She tried to catch her breath, but the intake and outflow of breath would not settle in her chest. She felt her heart pounding. She placed her hand on her chest, feeling its insistent thump through her ribcage. To her, the rhythm sounded like the battle beat of drums, but instead of dying down, her heart pounded all the more insistently. "Calm yourself," she said to the evergreen air. But instead of calm, her vision narrowed as her head pounded.

She cried out then. Gave wind to her weeping. "Help! Help! Help!" she cried, but her words echoed off the trees.

And then, a presence. "Hagar, Sarai's servant," said a voice from beside her.

It didn't sound like the tenor of a man, nor did it trill as a woman's. Deep, resonant. Hagar made herself turn toward the voice, hoping her narrowed eyesight would return to normal. She saw a figure there, then gasped at its height. Was she having a vision?

The figure stood before her now, and his skin glowed like the shimmer of a full moon at harvest. "Where have you come from, and where are you going?" he asked.

What could she say? Was there a correct answer to this question? Was this a trick of Sarai's, sending this man to test her? She let out the breath she held, took in another, and opted for truth. "I'm running away from my mistress, Sarai," she replied.

As she uttered these words of truth, she realized this was no man who stood before her near the spring of water. He was an angel. She'd heard of these apparitions in Egypt, visions of the warriors of the God of all gods, but she had never encountered them. Until this moment, she had thought them myths.

"Return to your mistress," the angel said, "and submit to her authority."

These were not the words Hagar wanted to hear. She groaned.

The angel looked at Hagar with compassion. "I will give you more descendants than you can count."

What could this mean? How could an apparition make such a promise? Hagar clasped her hands around her swollen belly.

"You are now pregnant and will give birth to a son."

A son? She thrilled at the thought. A son!

"You are to name him Ishmael...for the LORD has heard your cry of distress," the angel said. "This son of your will be a wild man, as untamed as a wild donkey! He will raise his fist against everyone, and everyone will be against him. Yes, he will live in open hostility against all his relatives."

Ishmael...God hears. *He* heard her cry for help, and now she would name her son Ishmael, "God hears." What could this mean? This was no angel who stood before her in pearlescence—it was God, the Creator of all she could see. She tried to think through His words about her son being wild and untamed, but her mind wouldn't fully grasp the meaning of the sentences. Instead, as the spring gurgled beside her, awe hushed her.

"El Roi," she finally said. "You are the God who sees me."

When Sarai mistreated her, the God who lived beyond the sky saw it all. When she fled into the wilderness? God took note of her. As her baby kicked his wild intentions on the walls of her womb, God knew.

"Have I truly seen the One who sees me?" she asked. But as she voiced her question, the looming figure evaporated, like mist, leaving her alone along the spring's edge.

Oh, but she was not alone. She was *seen*.

Hagar took a ribbon from her hair, scarlet under a new sky, and tied it around the trunk of the tree she'd once backed up against. She named the place Beer-lahai-roi, "well of the Living One who sees me." Instead of venturing away from the place toward Bered, she turned around and obeyed the voice of the One who saw her and headed toward Kadesh…and Sarai.

Sarai continued her abuse, but Hagar endured it, knowing God saw it all. As her time grew near, and she screamed Eve's pain into the blue sky, praying for relief, a son cried his way into their encampment—baby Ishmael. He cried so loudly that Hagar did believe God heard. She presented this untamed boy to Abram, now eighty-six but young in his joy for this son of his.

Thirteen years Hagar endured Sarai's anger. Thirteen years of unsteady conversations and innuendos. Hagar comforted herself as she remembered her encounter with the God who Sees, but each day, the memory felt farther and farther away, like a moving oasis. Had it actually happened?

Abram by now had trod ninety-nine years on the sunbaked earth, and God had yet to answer his prayer for a child from Sarai's womb. Hagar wondered if perhaps Ishmael would be his only son. She hoped so. This fact secured her safety and promised blessing and inheritance for Ishmael.

But then one day Hagar felt the Presence she'd experienced by the spring in the wilderness. From afar, she saw the Lord appear before Abram. She crept behind the nearest tent to hear what was said, then wondered if perhaps God would turn and speak to her?

"I am El-Shaddai—God Almighty," God said. His voice thundered and sang, both melody and harmony. It made Hagar nearly weep with longing.

Abram bowed in the dust, his head bent beneath the sun.

"Serve me faithfully and live a blameless life."

Abram nodded but said nothing.

"I will make a covenant with you, by which I will guarantee to give you countless descendants."

Abram no longer kneeled. Instead, he kissed the dust of the ground. Prostrate.

"This is My covenant with you: I will make you the father of a multitude of nations!"

Hagar wondered what this meant. Hadn't God told her that Ishmael would father many?

"What's more, I am changing your name. It will no longer be Abram. Instead, you will be called Abraham, for you will be the father of many nations. I will make you extremely fruitful. Your descendants will become many nations, and kings will be among them!"

Abram-now-Abraham remained on the ground.

"I will confirm My covenant with you and your descendants after you, from generation to generation," the Lord continued. "This is the everlasting covenant: I will always be your God and the God of your descendants after you. And I will give the entire land of Canaan, where you now live as a foreigner, to you and your descendants. It will be their possession forever, and I will be their God."

As Abraham continued lying in the dust, the Lord spoke of the covenant's sign—circumcision. He finished, "Your bodies will bear the mark of My everlasting covenant. Any male who fails to be circumcised will be cut off from the family for breaking the covenant."

Hagar wondered at these words. Would Ishmael suffer under the knife?

God continued, turning his attention to Sarai, as Abram-turned-Abraham kissed the earth.

"From now on," He said, "her name will be Sarah. And I will bless her and give you a son from her! Yes, I will bless her richly, and she will become the mother of many nations. Kings of nations will be among her descendants."

Oh, dear God, no. Hagar felt the weight of God's words in her heart. Ishmael would have a half-brother through Sarai-turned-Sarah. What would become of them?

Abraham roused himself from the ground, then bowed again. Hagar heard him laugh.

He must be thinking about the ridiculousness of this promise, she thought.

"May Ishmael live under your special blessing!" he proclaimed.

Hagar felt relief, finally. Ishmael was Abraham's son. Surely he would be known as that forever, right?

But God, the God who Sees, said no. A new son would come—Isaac, Sarah's long-awaited child. Ishmael would be blessed, but his blessing would pale in comparison to his younger brother's, though he would become the father of twelve princes.

At that, God left. Hagar felt His absence like a slap. And just as quickly as He left, Abraham took Ishmael, along with all the other males in his household, fashioned a flint knife, and cut the foreskin from her son.

A year later, in Abraham's hundredth year, ninety-year-old Sarah herself screamed Eve's curse toward a cloudy sky. Isaac reigned as the heir apparent, and the world tilted beneath Hagar's feet.

Isaac grew up as a prince, nursing at his mother's ancient breast. As he suckled his last, Abraham swelled with pride and prepared a feast to celebrate the milestone. Though Hagar had cautioned her wild-headed son to use decorum and caution—they were living on borrowed time, she knew—he bent toward mockery just as she had done in her foolish youth. And once Ishmael began, no one could stop his flow of words. He teased his younger brother in the presence of Sarah, the protector, at the very celebration of his weaning.

Sarah, fury in her eyes, turned toward Abraham. "Get rid of that slave woman and her son," she hissed. "He is not going to share the inheritance with my son, Isaac. I won't have it!" Abraham melted beneath his wife's words. Hagar knew he did not want to forsake his firstborn. He had told her as much.

The next morning, early as sunrise, Abraham awakened Hagar and Ishmael. He handed her provisions and a jar of water. With care, he strapped both to Hagar's tired shoulders. He pointed toward the wilderness of Beersheba and said nothing, but she understood what he meant. *Go. Leave. Begone.*

This time, she had no aim. Her footsteps made circular pathways in the sand, moving forward, backward, sideways, and confused. Though Hagar rationed their water, a day came when it dried clear up. She found a bush and told fourteen-year-old Ishmael to rest in its shade, then she walked ten stones' throws away. "I don't want to watch the boy die," she said as she burst into tears.

The God who named Ishmael "God hears" heard her cries in the wilderness once again. From the heavens, an angel called to her, "Hagar, what's wrong?"

Couldn't he see what was wrong? They would both die!

"Do not be afraid! God has heard the boy crying as he lies there. Go to him and comfort him, for I will make a great nation from his descendants."

At that moment, Hagar's eyes opened as if for the first time. There before her stood a well, overflowing with water. She quickly filled her container and gave the boy a drink.

The Biblical Narrative

You can find Hagar's story in Genesis 16 and 21.

There are a lot of firsts in this passage about Hagar. She is the first person in the Bible to be visited by an angel. She is the first to give God a name. The promise God gave to Abraham has echoes of similar language: "I will multiply." She expresses the most emotion thus far in the biblical story when she sees her son dying. She is the first person in the Bible to openly weep. Later, we read that she (as a mother) finds a wife for her son, Ishmael. This is the only time in the Bible a mother secures a mate for her son. She is the progenitor of the Ishmaelites who migrated to central and northern Arabia. Later in the story arc, it is the Ishmaelite traders who purchase young Joseph, whose transportation to Egypt leads to Israel's deliverance from famine.

Hagar experienced two aspects of God: His ears and His eyes. He heard her cry. He saw her plight. But He did not stand aloof from this exiled slave. Here you see the heart of God for all the people of the world, not simply His chosen people. Even as the nation of Israel was formed through Isaac, the promised child, God chose to simultaneously bless a foreign, single mother whose name can be translated in numerous ways: "flight," "other," "outsider," "stranger," and "who let her in?" In short, Hagar was misunderstood, maligned, and seemingly forgotten. But God did not forget her.

Not only that, but Hagar's life serves as a foreshadowing of what would come. She herself left Egypt, much like the nation of Israel would flee from there generations later. Her life projected even farther in the future when she also unknowingly mimicked Abraham's later journey into the wilderness with Isaac, potentially to sacrifice him on an altar at God's request. Just as she wept for the plight of her thirsty Ishmael, Abraham would face the possible death of Isaac. Both boys were gloriously delivered through supernaturally natural means—Ishmael through the appearance of a well, Isaac through the appearance of a ram caught in a thicket. Peering toward the New Testament period, we hear the foreshadowing of the angel Gabriel's words when he proclaimed that Mary would bear a son.

Later in the New Testament, the Apostle Paul uses Hagar as a metaphor for slavery when he writes,

The Scriptures say that Abraham had two sons, one from his slave wife and one from his freeborn wife. The son of the slave wife was born in a human attempt to bring about the fulfillment of God's promise. But the son of the freeborn wife was born as God's fulfillment of his promise. These two women serve as an illustration of God's two covenants. The first woman, Hagar, represents Mount Sinai where people received the law that enslaved them. And now Jerusalem is just like Mount Sinai in Arabia, because she and her children live in slavery to the law. (Galatians 4:22–25)

Note that this is not necessarily an indictment against Hagar. She had no volition to create her circumstance. In many ways, this confirms her slavery—yet even still the Law is compared to her. Remember what Jesus said about the Law in Matthew 5:17–18: "Don't misunderstand why I have come. I did not come to abolish the law of Moses or the writings of the prophets. No, I came to accomplish their purpose. I tell you the truth, until heaven and earth disappear, not even the smallest detail of God's law will disappear until its purpose is achieved."

The Law was part of God's great redemptive plan. And as we compare it to Hagar, we see she is part of that plan as well; she is seen and heard by God, even visited by Him. Her offspring would rescue Joseph, as I mentioned earlier, securing the nation's future. And as we consider the New Covenant, she represents those who would be brought into the fold through the blood of Jesus Christ, where "there is no longer Jew or Gentile, slave or free, male and female. For you are all one in Christ Jesus" (Galatians 3:28).

As the Apostle Paul finishes his argument about enslavement and the freedom he longs to see in every believer, he continues, "And you, dear brothers and sisters, are children of the promise, just like Isaac. But you are now being persecuted by those who want you to keep the law, just as Ishmael, the child born by human effort, persecuted Isaac, the child born by the power of the Spirit" (Galatians 4:28–29).

The principle here is this: those who are free are often persecuted by those who are not—out of jealousy or anger. This is an important truth for those of us who feel misunderstood: perhaps we are misunderstood precisely because we are children of promise, steeped in freedom. Again, this is not condemnation of Hagar per se; it is simply the illustration Paul uses to portray a powerful truth.

He continues, summarizing Hagar's plight: "But what do the Scriptures say about that? 'Get rid of the slave and her son, for the son of the slave woman will not share the inheritance with the free woman's son.' So, dear brothers and sisters, we are not children of the slave woman; we are children of the free woman" (Galatians 4:30–31). Though Hagar is dismissed and sent into the wilderness, as we saw in the earlier narrative, God does not forsake her, but preserves both her and her offspring. What a testimony to His ability to take notice of the banished and broken!

Because of Hagar's lack of rights (to put her plight in modern terms), she could not help her situation other than to call out to God in desperation. And God intervened. Though hers was not a son of promise but of a human attempt to fulfill the promises of God, he was nonetheless blessed and cared for.

How This Applies to Misunderstood You

Hagar's misunderstanding comes in her humanity. In her culture of enslavement, she would never be understood except in terms of property. Her very humanity was disregarded when Sarai forced her to sleep with her master, Abram. Not a person but a pawn, Hagar had no choice but to comply—just as a horse must obey rein and bit. This kind of powerful misunderstanding permeates our culture today, though our own pride blinds us from believing this to be true.

Whenever we demean another person because of their skin color, immigration status, seeming lack of intelligence, poverty, or differing political belief, we are guilty of misunderstanding the *imago dei* of the other. Before we look at how others misunderstand us, we have to turn the lens on ourselves, asking difficult questions. *Am I prejudiced? Do I look down upon those who differ from me? Do I consider some people less-than?* Jesus reminds us that the Kingdom boils down to two commands: love Him; love others. And often our lack of love for others reveals our lack of love for the God who created everyone. The Apostle John puts it in stark terms: "If someone says, 'I love God,' but hates a fellow believer, that person is a liar; for if we don't love people we can see, how can we love God whom we cannot see?" (1 John 4:20). The question becomes: when do we love misunderstanding others? When do we relish it? When is it easy for us to do? And why?

After that self-reflection, we have a better understanding of our own battles with misunderstanding. Why? Because we now understand how we've hurt others. To repent of that kind of prejudgment doesn't merely mean acknowledging our sin, but diving into empathy— choosing to feel someone's else's pain in being misunderstood. Easy repentance does not dive into the pain we have caused another. It simply glosses over it, refusing to acknowledge the carnage our words or actions have wrought. But true repentance means stepping into the hurt we have caused, living it, and then penitently asking the person and our God for forgiveness. Only then do we have the headspace to consider our own pain of being misunderstood.

I write this because I know my tendency. It's easy for me to make myself the blighted hero who endures the punishment of others without first acknowledging how I've hurt people. But the more we choose to honestly pray, "Search me, O God, and know my heart; test me and know my anxious thoughts. Point out anything in me that offends you, and lead me along the path of everlasting life" (Psalm 139:23–24), the better we will understand that every human being hurts others. We are not special or above it. To make ourselves the sole victim of humanity's tyranny is to live a dishonest life. We have sinned. We have slayed others with our words. We have misunderstood many.

Once we have walked through our own repentance journey, we can take time to acknowledge our own pain. In fact, walking the forgiveness road with honesty attunes us to our need for the Lord when we are misunderstood. And in that place, Hagar offers us concrete encouragement. We do not see her appealing to those who enslaved her. She does not argue or strive to change her circumstance, though she does take to looking down on Sarah (she is not immune to sin). Instead, when she finds herself overcome by her circumstances, she cries out to God. She gives full vent to her emotions and anguish. She literally has nowhere else to turn. No friend. No family member other than Ishmael in her second exile. No country. Nothing.

Have you ever felt that way? Have you ever felt stripped of relationships and home? Have you come to that place where others have misunderstood you to the point of exile? This is why Hagar's response in such a broken situation helps us. When zero people come to our rescue, when we are alone, we, like Hagar, can turn to the God who hears us and sees our predicament. Like the psalmist, we can cry, "Whom have I in heaven but you? I desire you more than anything on earth. My health may fail, and my spirit may grow weak, but God remains the strength of my heart; he is mine forever" (Psalm 73:25–26).

Hagar reminds us that God hears. The Psalms are full of God's promises to hear our cries, including this one: "But God did listen! He paid attention to my prayer. Praise God, who did not ignore my prayer or withdraw his unfailing love from me" (Psalm 66:19–20). Proverbs 15:29 reminds us of this truth as well: "The LORD is far from the wicked, but he hears the prayers of the righteous." What a powerful truth, particularly when we look back at Hagar. God heard her desperate cry and answered her—which means that He saw her as worthy of being answered. Jesus similarly reminds us, "We know that God doesn't listen to sinners, but he is ready to hear those who worship him and do his will" (John 9:31).

When we face misunderstanding in our humanity (when we are dismissed, maligned, or relegated to the back seat of life), we can rest in knowing that God not only hears our cries, but sees our predicament. We are reminded of God's eyes upon us in 2 Chronicles 16:9a, "The eyes of the LORD search the whole earth in order to strengthen those whose hearts are fully committed to him."

When we feel utterly alone, God sees us. He longs to strengthen us in our frailty. He also sees correctly. His vision is perfect. He sees beyond appearances and looks into the heart. This is particularly comforting when you're suffering at the hands of someone who appears to be righteous. God gave Samuel this important advice when He chose David as king: "Don't judge by his appearance or height, for I have rejected him. The Lord doesn't see things the way you see them. People judge by outward appearance, but the Lord looks at the heart" (1 Samuel 16:7). Later, King David reminds his son Solomon, "For the Lord sees every heart and knows every plan and thought" (1 Chronicles 28:9). In David's final prayer before the entire assembly of Israel, he reiterates, "I know, my God, that you examine our hearts and rejoice when you find integrity there" (1 Chronicles 29:17). That God sees us is both a comfort and a conundrum. He may see our integrity, and He may see areas of sin and growth we need to confront. To welcome the gaze of God is to welcome both.

Solomon referred to the ears and eyes of God as he dedicated the Temple. "O my God, may your eyes be open and your ears attentive to all the prayers made to you in this place" (2 Chronicles 6:40). In the New Testament, Peter summarizes God's ability to hear and see us in 1 Peter 3:12: "The eyes of the Lord watch over those who do right, and his ears are open to their prayers. But the Lord turns his face against those who do evil."

This is perhaps the most comforting verse for the misunderstood and maligned. As Creator of all, the Fashioner of all humankind's hearts, He knows everything. He sees all nuance, all motives, all aspects of each interaction. Because of His omniscience and superior intelligence, He judges correctly—even when others cannot see.

I'm reminded of a friend who was preyed upon by a seemingly stellar Christian leader. She raised the alarm and shared what happened—but only after he had continued to harass her. The Christian world turned on her, spewing vicious words her way. How dare she harm the reputation of the stellar leader? Through heartache, quietness, and trust, she persisted, though it cost her nearly everything. A couple of years later, though, everything came out. All that she had shared was true, and the leader everyone supported turned out to be a wolf in sheep's clothing. Jesus reminds us, "For all that is secret will eventually be brought into the open, and everything that is concealed will be brought to light and be made known to all" (Luke 8:17).

What happens, though, when it appears God does not see? What if that Christian leader had never been exposed? That's when eschatological living becomes vital. To live in light of the Kingdom is to remember there will be a day of recompense. Not a single human being will escape the holy gaze of the Omniscient One. All will be made right. Justice will prevail. I have experienced this delayed gratification many times. Some who have harmed me have passed to glory. Though they seemed to easily escape earthly justice, they will not escape divine justice in the New Heaven and the New Earth. (This reminds me, though, that I too am in utter need of a savior. Without Christ, I would face the same exposing judgment. I could not stand before a holy God.)

Hagar teaches us that God hears and sees when we are misunderstood. These twin rock-solid truths can bring us a settled peace as we navigate what is next.

Truths about Fully Understood You

- God sees you, even when you feel unnoticed or forgotten.
- When you pray, God hears you.
- God knows how to provide for your every need.
- Your perseverance in the things of God matters for eternity.
- You can rest in God's sovereign judgment and plan.

Questions for Discussion

1. What stands out to you in the fictionalized account of Hagar's story?
2. Sarai had a difficult, contentious relationship that did not resolve itself in her lifetime. How do you relate to that?
3. God visits Hagar not once, but twice. He reassures her of His presence in desperate situations. How has God visited you in your desperation?
4. Hagar's name means "flight." Why do you think it's tempting to flee when life takes a difficult turn? When have you fled your circumstances? What happened when you did?
5. Hagar persevered through many trials. How does her example help you face your current worries? How does God's reality and presence empower you to take the next step?

CHAPTER THREE

Leah, the Unlovely One

Though the oldest daughter of Laban, Leah lived under the specter of her sister Rachel's beauty. Fellow shepherds bowed their eyes as Rachel passed by. Women clucked their approval, speculating about who would capture such a beauty, as Leah looked on with weakened eyes. Leah could hope for nothing more than a marriage of convenience, where an alliance hitched together important families. She would never be desired—not as Rachel was.

When Jacob entered their encampment, Leah took note of the spark in Rachel's eyes. Jacob, his eyes still wet from tears, hastily explained his lineage. Her father embraced and kissed the kinsman and exclaimed, "You really are my own flesh and blood!"

Jacob, slick-backed and hale, worked under the sun's gaze for four Sabbaths. He toiled with joy, Leah thought. And that's when she dared to hope that she, the firstborn daughter, would be given in alliance—to enmesh their families together. She took note of his form, the work of his hands, the way he coddled the sheep and goats in his care, and she let herself dream of a future outside the confines of her stifling home.

Near a stand of mandrakes, Leah overheard her father tell Jacob, "You shouldn't work for me without pay just because we are relatives. Tell me how much your wages should be."

Leah, always smart with compensation, calculated what Jacob should ask for—a game she often played to pass the time in the affairs of her homestead.

When Jacob opened his mouth, she expected him to ask for a four-Sabbath wage. But no numbers left his mouth. "I'll work for you for seven years if you'll give me Rachel, your younger daughter, as my wife."

Leah's world collapsed amid the mandrakes. She sucked in a breath, let it out. Told herself not to weep. But logic steadied her in the silence between the men. Surely her father would remind Jacob of their traditions. *A younger sibling should not marry before the older. It's not the way things are done. Why doesn't Jacob understand that? Why has he come to disrupt the social order of things? Father will rebuke Jacob for such a ridiculous request.*

But her father's words hammered her to the earth. "Agreed!"

Agreed? Has he forgotten all tradition?

Father gestured over all his land. He smiled. "I'd rather give her to you than to anyone else. Stay and work with me."

Leah collapsed inside herself. She would be an old maid, supplanted by her younger, more beautiful sister. She would be relegated to this barren land under Father's gaze for the rest of her earthly life.

Her only hope lay in time. Seven years of labor Father had eked out of Jacob. Perhaps in that scope of years, a suitor would wander onto their land and see the unique beauty Leah had to offer—her intelligence, wit, and compassion.

But seven years produced no such matrimony.

In the same stand of mandrakes where Father and Jacob struck their agreement, Jacob reminded him, "I have fulfilled my agreement. Now give me my wife so I can sleep with her."

Clans, workers, and people in the nearby village came to celebrate the familial affair. Leah had been tasked with food preparation, for there were lambs to slaughter and cook, bread to knead and bake, and wine to proffer for the celebration. She dutifully worked through tears alongside her servant Zilpah, trying not to betray her brokenness. After the festivities, as the nighttime claimed the day, in the pitch dark with no moon to cast light, Father approached and told her to follow him.

His grip upon her forearm felt forceful, and his hand dug into her flesh. He mumbled about the proper way of things as he led her toward Jacob's tent. Beneath her veil, she gasped. What was he doing? Though she wanted matrimony, she did not want it through deception. But before she knew it, Jacob's rough hands held the sides of arms, as he drew her toward him in the bedded tent. "Rachel, my love," he said as he pulled her into a fierce embrace.

Her first kiss took place in the dark under pretense, but in that moment, she felt more wanted than at any time in her life. Though she dreaded Jacob's face in the morning, she succumbed to his desire, matching it with her own. In the night she heard her husband—*her husband!*—breathing. She could not make out the contours of his face, but her hands traced over his shoulders as he slept. Seven years of hard labor had quieted him, producing the deepest of sleeps. Leah knew that these last midnight hours would give way to light, and everything would change. She asked God to hold the sun back from shining, but dawn came, and with that, a yawp from Jacob's mouth.

"Leah!" He spat her name like a swear word, his eyes laced with betrayal and wrath. Though she had not connived her way into the tent, he believed that to be the case—and his actions confirmed it.

He raged out of the tent. Leah pulled on her tunic, wrapped her head in a veil, and stood outside in the day's harsh light. Rachel ran to her. "How could you do such a thing?" she asked. But Leah had no words. It mattered not what she said—even if her words had the convincing power of a seer, everyone knew that Father's sentences would win the argument. She would forever be known as the usurper.

Jacob shouted for Father, who eventually emerged from his tent. "What have you done to me?" His voice sounded like the roar of a lion. "I worked seven years for Rachel!" He looked over at the two sisters, glancing beyond Leah as if she were a stone in his path, and settled into Rachel's aching gaze. "Why have you tricked me?"

Leah knew of the trickery of Jacob, how he had absconded with his brother's birthright and stolen his blessing before coming to their farm. What an odd accusation: he had only experienced what he had done to his own brother. Leah smiled at the irony.

"It's not our custom here to marry off a younger daughter ahead of the firstborn," her father replied. "But wait until the bridal week is over; then we'll give you Rachel, too—provided you promise to work another seven years for me."

Leah felt the abandonment already, could sense Jacob's distaste for her. He tolerated her during the bridal week, while she nursed her pain. And one Sabbath later, it was Rachel who stepped inside the tent and experienced what Leah had only known in pretense.

Four Sabbaths later, Leah's stomach recoiled at the curds the herd had provided that day. After she wiped her mouth from vomiting in the field, she smiled. Surely Jacob would love her now because she would produce the first heir. She waited several sunrises before she told him. "I am with child," she said. For a hesitant moment, she could see light in his countenance.

"This is good news," he said. But then he turned to Rachel, whose gaze was directed heavenward. "You will be next," he said.

Except that Rachel was not.

Reuben yelped into the world, the pride of Leah. "Look, a son!" she said. "The LORD has noticed my misery." His name communicated her hope that one day Jacob would recognize her as his first wife, and his love for her would grow. She spent her days mothering Reuben, tending to the home, and helping out wherever she could in order to gain Jacob's gaze or favor. There were moments when Jacob's desire for another child overshadowed his distaste for her. Leah learned to accept any level of affection Jacob doled out, and in that uneasy alliance, a small camaraderie emerged like a weed from between rocks. Even so, Jacob made it clear he had only one true love—Rachel, the barren one.

Simeon hollered his way onto the soil of Paddan-Aram next. His name was a cry of anguish—Leah remained in her unloved state, and God had taken note of her plight, rewarding her with offspring. As she looked at Simeon's sweet face, she consoled herself with the truth that God heard her cry.

Levi followed. Leah named him thus in hopes that a third son would finally gain Jacob's attention—that he would finally attach himself to her and find a reserve of affection to send her way. But his attentiveness was spent on Rachel's tears.

Judah did not cry at his birth. His eyes widened at the earth around him as if in astonishment. For four years, Leah had fought through her plight. Though she named her pain to no one but her breastfeeding boys and the Lord who provided them, the outworking of grief ended in settled *shalom*. Though unloved and unwanted, she knew God would be with her. Judah's name was a proclamation of her journey. "Now I will praise the LORD!" she declared to the stars.

Leah watched as Rachel's barrenness turned to anxiety, then grief, then desperation. She yelled, "Give me children, or I'll die!" in Jacob's direction.

Leah finally saw impatience in Jacob's eyes, an exasperation she hoped would help him see how faithful *she* had been. Surely, she would not speak to him as harshly.

"Am I God?" he asked. "He's the one who has kept you from having children!"

That's when Rachel mimicked Jacob's grandmother's choice, presenting Bilhah to Jacob as Sarai had offered Hagar. The next year,

Bilhah presented the resulting baby to Rachel, who named him Dan—a boy whose name meant that God had vindicated her barrenness. Naphtali came next, and Rachel smiled. In Leah's presence, she said, "I have struggled hard with my sister, and I'm winning!"

This sparked a competitive streak in Leah, a longing to come out ahead not only in the child count, but in Jacob's affections as well. She copied Sarai's tactic as well, offering Zilpah to her husband. Gad, a boy whose name meant good fortune, came next. Asher followed, and with his pronouncement, Leah said, "What joy is mine! Now the other women will celebrate with me."

Reuben, working bare-chested in the emmer fields, burst through the entrance to Leah's tent. "Look what I found," he said. He presented her with choice mandrakes. "Now you can give birth again!" Leah rejoiced that God had taken notice of her secondary infertility and found a way to change everything. Everyone knew that mandrakes sparked fertility.

But Rachel got wind of Leah's fortune. She entered the tent after Reuben, eyes desperate in the way that only one who has experienced complete barrenness can know, and approached Leah. "Please give me some of your son's mandrakes."

Leah caught Rachel's intense gaze and felt the bile rise in her throat. Rachel, who had the affection of Jacob. Rachel, who now held two sons of her handmaiden. Rachel, who lived on the earth as an honored beauty. She had everything, and Leah had nothing—at least, nothing of the love she wanted. "Wasn't it enough that you stole my husband?" she snapped. "Now you will steal my son's mandrakes, too?"

Tears leapt from Rachel's eyes, and Leah almost felt compassion. "I will let Jacob sleep with you tonight if you give me some of the mandrakes."

Leah agreed. That evening, as Jacob returned from the fields, she approached him. "You must come and sleep with me tonight!"

Jacob gave her a confused look and then scanned the horizon, seemingly lost in thought.

"I have paid for you with some mandrakes that my son found," she said.

That evening, Leah smiled as they consummated under a desert sky. And as she lay there, she prayed God would answer her plea for an opened womb. God graciously answered her cry. Issachar, the boy whose name meant "reward," entered their world, followed by Zebulun, the one she hoped would elicit long-awaited honor from Jacob. The Lord God had rewarded her thrice with the dawning of Dinah, a daughter whose eyes resembled Jacob's.

It was then that the Lord saw fit to hear the longstanding cries of her sister, Rachel. Her belly swelled for nine months as Jacob doted on her. The joy between them soured Leah's heart, though she prayed she would learn to forgive and let go of her animosity. They were sisters, after all, born from the same father and mother, eking out a living on their father's harsh land. She finally understood: they needed each other.

Rachel wailed as the baby came, but then a baby's cry replaced hers.

She presented him to the family, pink-faced and content. "God has removed my disgrace. I present to you baby Joseph!" And with that proclamation, the baby opened his eyes and looked upon his mother. Rachel, captivated, said, "May the LORD add yet another son to my family."

Jacob's work ethic and God's faithfulness brought reward— livestock, wealth, offspring. His time under Laban's tyranny came to an end when the Lord God appeared to him in a dream. Jacob later recounted the story to his wives. God said to him, "I am the God who appeared to you at Bethel, the place where you anointed the pillar of stone and made your vow to Me. Now get ready to leave this country and return to the land of your birth."

For once, Leah felt like all of them were a family—a phenomenon birthed from their father's iron fist and impertinent demands. Leah lifted her weary eyes to see the place of the sun's setting, daydreaming of what could be. Would freedom lie beyond her gaze? Would their family finally experience the *shalom* of God once they left everything they knew? Hope rose within her. She conferred with Rachel as she nursed baby Joseph. Together they agreed.

"That's fine with us!" Leah told Jacob, grateful that he wanted their input in such a critical family decision. "We won't inherit any of our father's wealth anyway. He has reduced our rights to those of foreign women. And after he sold us, he wasted the money you paid him for us. All the wealth God has given you from our father legally belongs to us and our children. So go ahead and do whatever God has told you."

They stole away toward the country of Gilead. Leah felt what had been an elusive emotion: joy. *Escape!* As she rode on a camel, her sons nearby, she set her face like flint toward what would come next. But soon the sound of galloping hooves rang behind them, and Father caught them all.

Leah wanted nothing to do with the man and had no need of goodbye, so when he waxed eloquent about his grief over them leaving, she shook her head. He only wanted their wealth, not a relationship. Still, Laban kept up with the jilted-father charade. "What do you mean by deceiving me like this? How dare you drag my daughters away like prisoners of war?"

Leah felt the irony in her stomach. There, in Paddan-Aram, she had been the prisoner. Now that she breathed free air, she longed for her father to stop talking. But he did not.

"Why did you slip away secretly? Why did you deceive me? And why didn't you say you wanted to leave? I would have given you a farewell feast, with singing and music, accompanied by tambourines and harps. Why didn't you let me kiss my daughters and grandchildren and tell them goodbye? You have acted very foolishly!" Their father got down from his steed, dusted himself off, and said, "I could destroy you, but the God of your father appeared to me last night and warned me, 'Leave Jacob alone!' I can understand your feeling that you must go, and your intense longing for your father's home. But why have you stolen my gods?"

Leah grimaced. She knew her sister had stolen the idols, hiding them as they stole away, then secreting them beneath her in the tent, using her monthly cycle as a ruse. What if Father found them? Would they have to abandon their journey and return to his grip?

But after a fruitless search for the gods and some back-and-forth between her husband and her father, they agreed to a covenant. They gathered stones, creating a pile they named *Galeed*, "Witness Pile." Laban gave it a secondary name: *Mizpah*, which meant "watch-tower." He proclaimed, "May the Lord keep watch between us to make sure that we keep this covenant when we are out of each other's sight. If you mistreat my daughters or if you marry other wives, God will see it even if no one else does. He is a witness to the covenant between us."

Jacob promised to respect the boundary between them. Father turned toward home, and Jacob's large family ventured toward Gilead.

When news of Jacob's estranged twin brother, Esau, reached the camp, Leah took note of Jacob's fear. He sent the entire family ahead of him, along with gifts for Esau. Leah bristled at the way he positioned each family—the two maidservants and their sons and daughters first, followed by her—then Rachel, the one he loved, the one he always protected and coddled.

But Leah held her head high because she could taste freedom in the air. She would be emancipated from her lot, set free to mother her children in an unfamiliar place—far from Father's gaze. As God delivered Jacob from the hand of Esau, she let out a breath, thanking Him for His care, marveling that, although she had married under pretense, she now had a family—one to whom, according to the stories passed down from Jacob's grandfather Abraham, God had promised a glorious destiny. Imagine her—the unlovely one—playing such an important role for the future of her people! She looked behind her as Rachel held Joseph's sweet hand and smiled.

Perhaps the greatest miracle was her deepening love for her sister.

The Biblical Narrative

Our culture favors the beautiful. This is a truth passed down through the ages—those who are attractive get farther in our world. It may not seem fair, but more often than not, beauty helps people win affection, esteem, and success. You can see the disparity in the meaning of each sister's name in this story. Rachel's means "ewe" or "young lamb." It's associated with purity. "Leah," by contrast, means "wild cow" and has connotations of weariness, which may explain what the Bible says about her eyes. According to Genesis 29:17, they lacked sparkle. Other translations say she was "tender-eyed" (KJV), "weak and dull-looking" (AMPC), "delicate" (CEV), or "bleary-eyed" (WYC). On the contrary, other translators interpret the Hebrew passage concerning her eyes differently. The GNT says her eyes were "lovely," while the HCSB says "ordinary." *The Message* says this: "Now Laban had two daughters; Leah was the older and Rachel the younger. Leah had nice eyes, but Rachel was stunningly beautiful."

Regardless of whether Leah was attractive or not, the Scriptures are clear that she was deemed inferior to her sister in external beauty. This beauty attracted Jacob to Rachel, yes, but would it sustain throughout the narrative?

It must be noted that both women were most likely used by their father to gain the blessing of having Jacob work his land. This financial alliance was for Laban's benefit, and when Jacob realized his trickery, it was Laban who conscripted his labor for seven more years. In short, both women were property to Laban—leverage for the sake of his own economic prosperity.

Still, we see Leah's spiritual transformation as she grapples with her new state in life—an unloved pawn in Laban's grab for wealth and power. Her journey toward wholeness is seen through the naming of her children. What we see in her is overt grief as she wrestles with what must seem like an unchangeable situation. Her husband loves another, and even when she does everything within her power to win his heart (have children), she finds she cannot control his affections.

Note her journey in naming her biological sons.

Reuben, "behold a son." *Perhaps Jacob will love me now.*

Simeon, "to hear." *Perhaps God has heard that I was unloved.*

Levi, "joined." *Perhaps now that there are three sons, Jacob will connect with me.*

Judah, "praise." *Now I will praise the Lord.*

Issachar, "hire." *God has paid me back favorably because of my distress.*

Zebulon, "to dwell." *I have a place in this family.*

Dinah, "judge." *I have been judged fairly.*

Leah serves as an example of what it means to process grief. We bargain, hoping that, somehow, we can change an outcome. When that outcome does not change, we cry out to God, hoping for His ear. We try to live a moral life, falsely believing that spirituality is a simple formula of "if I do this, then God is obligated to do that."

When all else fails, when our world falls apart despite our best efforts, we come to a crisis point. Will we trust God or give up? Leah chose the former. She praised God in the midst of her messy life. From that mindset of praise, we see her reorient her focus from her circumstances toward her Creator. She sees that God rewards her, demonstrating the words of the writer of Hebrews: "And it is impossible to please God without faith. Anyone who wants to come to him must believe that God exists and that he rewards those who sincerely seek him" (11:6). She ends by finding her place in the world—as a follower of God, a wife, a mother, vindicated by the one true Judge, God Himself.

When Leah and Rachel flee with Jacob, take note of who steals Laban's idols. It was Leah, not Rachel who remained faithful to God. And when Leah dies, she is buried next to Jacob in the cave at *Qiryat-Arba*, while Rachel is buried on the side of the road en route to Bethlehem. Perhaps this indicates a final affection on Jacob's part, though it may also have been the only option available while the family was migrating over such a long distance.

At the beginning of Genesis, we are told marriage is intended to be between one man and one woman. "This explains why a man leaves his father and mother and is joined to his wife, and the two are united into one" (Genesis 2:24). Jacob disregarded the design of monogamous marriage when he chose to "marry" Rachel after he had already been joined to Leah. In light of that, we must be careful not to place blame on either wife for the sins of their husband. In their culture, they had few rights, and we see just how poorly Laban treated them. Later, when the Law was introduced, Moses warned of the very thing Jacob was caught up in: "While your wife is living, do not marry her sister and have sexual relations with her, for they would be rivals" (Leviticus 18:18).

Leah had seven children (including Dinah), the number of perfection. Rachel had two. Their combined concubines birthed four, making the twelve tribes of Israel. This nation would be God's city on a hill, wooing the world to Himself. While unloved, Leah persevered in her life, producing the most heirs. Later in the Book of Ruth, Leah and Rachel are invoked as a blessing. "Then the elders and all the people standing in the gate replied, 'We are witnesses! May the LORD make this woman who is coming into your home like Rachel and Leah, from whom all the nation of Israel descended! May you prosper in Ephrathah and be famous in Bethlehem'" (Ruth 4:11).

And as we trace the lineage of Jesus Christ, we can't help but marvel at God's kindness to Leah. It was through her child Judah that Christ would come into our world. Her trust in God's willingness to work through her pain ended in praise, and that praise-of-a-son would bring the greatest gift of salvation to our world.

How This Applies to Misunderstood You

Leah's misunderstanding comes from being judged for her outward appearance. Her dismissal is something she cannot control, no matter how hard she tries. This is a difficult misunderstanding, and it's rampant in our world. Those who are deemed attractive make more money, find greater success, and have more opportunities. Our world rewards those who conform to social norms and dismisses those who don't.

The only way to work through this kind of unfair misunderstanding is to reorient our hearts and minds toward the reality of the Kingdom of God. Jesus reminded the disciples, "So those who are last now will be first then, and those who are first will be last" (Matthew 20:16). Appearances are deceptive. We've established already that God doesn't see as we see—His vision sees clear to the heart and its intentions. He chooses unlikely heroes throughout Scripture to carry out His purposes. You often see God choosing the younger sibling, the smallest tribe, the least likely, and the outcast to bring forth surprising victory. This is good news! It is the hope of the broken, the surprise of the lowly, the joy of the overlooked. Search the Scriptures with diligence, and you will find all sorts of hints of God's very different Kingdom math.

Leah, the unloved one, is the progenitor of the Messiah who loved the entire world.

My life verse echoes this paradox. I grew up as a ragamuffin, neglected, overlooked, harmed, and broken by trauma. I am still confounded that God looked from Heaven and decided to save the likes of me. Logically, it made no sense. I was not attractive, had a wreck of a home life, and possessed no real skills other than the ability to write a sentence or two. I can picture Him saying these words over me as I considered my worthlessness prior to meeting Him:

> Remember, dear brothers and sisters, that few of you were wise in the world's eyes or powerful or wealthy when God called you. Instead, God chose things the world considers foolish in order to shame those who think they are wise. And he chose things that are powerless to shame those who are powerful. God chose things despised by the world, things counted as nothing at all, and used them to bring to nothing what the world considers important. As a result, no one can ever boast in the presence of God. (1 Corinthians 1:26–29)

This is God's beautiful redemption. Not that we make ourselves presentable, or that our appearance gains us entrance—no, instead His heart is to redeem those who know their powerlessness, who understand their despised state, who feel as if they are nothing in a world of Everythings. We can either grieve our shortcomings and settle them before our ever-powerful God as Leah did, or we can sink into despair. Those of us who've been misunderstood in this way must remember that our broken places are the best places to experience God's turnaround. Our lack is a blessing. Our seeming hopelessness is an avenue to experience the hope of God.

Do people judge you based on your past? Do others dismiss you because of your economic state? Do some overlook you because of your appearance? It's their worldly vision that does so, not their Kingdom insight. Will those misunderstandings sideline you? Perhaps. Will harsh words hurt you? Of course. But it's important that we don't base our feelings of worth on the worthless chatter of the world. This world's systems are fickle. They are Darwinian, favoring the fittest over the broken. But God's upside-down Kingdom is utterly *other*. In His Kingdom, little is much, the last is first, and the unlikely is likely.

When we are unloved because of things we cannot control, when we are traumatized by others' malevolent intent, when we are deemed inferior because of the world's lopsided meritocracy, we can regroup by reminding ourselves that this world will pass away. We can remember that God rewards those who seek Him. Remember, "Anyone who wants to come to him must believe that God exists and that he rewards those who sincerely seek him" (Hebrews 11:6). We can stand on the truth that the weak are made strong precisely because they understand their weakness and their need for a savior.

Even if every person on this earth misunderstood us, we have an advocate in the Holy Spirit, a comforter who comforts us in all afflictions, a constant companion who loves to remind us of our status as children of the most high God. His ways are not like the world's. He thinks differently, acts differently, loves differently than we expect. Isaiah wrote, "'My thoughts are nothing like your thoughts,' says the Lord. 'And my ways are far beyond anything you could imagine. For just as the heavens are higher than the earth, so my ways are higher than your ways and my thoughts higher than your thoughts'" (Isaiah 55:8–9).

Later, the Apostle Paul echoes Isaiah 64:4 as a promise to us: "That is what the Scriptures mean when they say, 'No eye has seen, no ear has heard, and no mind has imagined what God has prepared for those who love him" (1 Corinthians 2:9). What a promise! What a way to live—in holy anticipation of what our paradoxical, surprising God can and will do in our lives.

Paul again reminds us of the Spirit within us. "And we have received God's Spirit (not the world's spirit), so we can know the wonderful things God has freely given us" (1 Corinthians 2:12). We do not think as the world does. We do not evaluate others on appearance or hearsay. Why? Because, as Paul concludes, "we understand these things, for we have the mind of Christ" (1 Corinthians 2:16b).

Friend, if you are maligned and misunderstood, there are two things you can do. The first is to remember that you have the mind of Christ, and you can discern how to endure harsh treatment, just as He did. The second is to let the pain of that misunderstanding develop your empathy muscle. Once you understand and experience that kind of pain, you'll be less likely to inflict it on others.

Later in 1 Corinthians 4:3, Paul comforts the misunderstood: "As for me, it matters very little how I might be evaluated by you or by any human authority. I don't even trust my own judgment on this point." Did you catch that? We can consider it inconsequential when others evaluate us wrongly. Security comes in understanding that God sees. He knows. He evaluates us perfectly. And when we're found lacking, we have the freedom to confess our shortcomings and walk away forgiven. That beautiful forgiveness then informs our behavior toward others. We can choose not to "make judgments about anyone ahead of time—before the Lord returns" (1 Corinthians 4:5).

You cannot change another's opinion of you, no matter how incorrect that opinion may be. You could spend your entire life trying to do so, but that would stifle your growth. It locks you into the past, robbing you of forward momentum and growth. Paul reminds us to forget what lies behind and to press on toward what lies ahead in the future (see Philippians 3:13). The only thing you can control is your obedience to God right now. As you obey Him, taking the next right step, you are moving toward that glorious future, and this demonstrates you have a growth mindset.

Will it hurt to have untethered and untrue opinions of you in the world? Yes, of course. But those opinions possess a malevolent malignancy *only when* you give them power by rehashing them and letting them worry your soul. The truth is: you are loved. The truth is: God sees you. The truth is: His opinion trumps all others. The truth is: you can, with God's Spirit within you, endure harsh treatment. You simply have to tap into the power available to you.

The Apostle Paul understood harsh judgment and treatment from enemies. He calls it "trouble" when he reflects on his time in Asia.

> We were crushed and overwhelmed beyond our ability to endure, and we thought we would never live through it. In fact, we expected to die. But as a result, we stopped relying on ourselves and learned to rely only on God, who raises the dead. And he did rescue us from mortal danger, and he will rescue us again. We have placed our confidence in him, and he will continue to rescue us. (2 Corinthians 1:8b–10)

Paul does not whitewash his circumstances, nor does he use platitudes to downplay their situation. He tells the truth, and then gives us all a nugget of wisdom: Trials and misunderstandings serve us. They reveal to us our need for rescue and strength from the only One who can offer it. Paul had no confidence in himself (see Philippians 3:3); instead, he placed his confidence in Christ—even when persecution could mean death.

Do not lose heart, oh misunderstood one. Others' incorrect opinions of you, their dismissal of your personhood—these cannot negate the very real truth of your belovedness. Made in the image of your Creator, you are loved and lovely. You are held and beheld. You are carried and cradled. You are rescued and redeemed. You are fought for and fortified. You are wanted and watered. You are chosen and cherished. You are delighted in and delivered. You are graced and granted God's precious promises. You can rest in that truth.

Truths about Fully Understood You

- You are beautiful because you bear the image of your Creator.
- God has a unique plan for you that may be surprising or unexpected.
- Even if you feel unloved by people, God deeply loves you.
- You, through your actions and fidelity to God, bring life and light to this earth.
- Your obedience matters for eternity.

Questions for Discussion

1. What new insights did you glean from Leah's story?
2. How does seeing a possible reconciliation between Leah and Rachel bring you hope in one of your broken relationships? What does it take to mend a difficult friendship or connection with a loved one?
3. In your life, what does it mean to obey God? What is He calling you to do? Why is it hard sometimes to obey Him?
4. What hope does Leah's story provide for you?
5. How does God demonstrate His care for Leah throughout this story? In the past five years, how has God specifically shown you that He loves you and takes note of your emotional needs?

CHAPTER FOUR

Rahab, the Prostituted One

The light gave way to early dusk as a swarm of mosquitoes sere-
naded Rahab's late-afternoon walk within the walls of Jericho.
She pulled in a steadying breath after she latched the outer door of her
home imbedded in the city's impenetrable fortress. This act of locking
would keep the riffraff out, though, truth be told, these were the same
people who supplied her family's sustenance. Though young, and
thought beautiful by some, she felt older than the stones of her city.
Who would pay her this evening? Would there be enough money to
provide a little more than a day's security? Her stomach rumbled—a
sign that she valued her family's fullness more than her own.

The air of Jericho tonight stilled. Rahab could feel something
indefinable just beyond her natural senses—as if the night marked a
turning point of some kind, and, from here on out, everything would
be different, though she had no idea what that could entail.

She looked again at the darkening azure sky above. Though her
culture was pagan, Rahab spent her days meditating on the cosmos.
While her neighbors accepted multiple gods as fact, she had always

been one to question those ideas. She couldn't simply accept their view of the world; her father had called her The Questioner since she was a toddler. Why would their world need multiple angry gods? And if these so-called gods were vengeful, why would they work together to produce this world? Wouldn't the sun god get angry at the moon god and snuff it out like a candlewick? And what of the god of thunder? Didn't he need the god of fertility's cooperation to send storms upon the earth?

No, the world she saw pointed to one Creator, one God, one Lawgiver. All that whispering from her neighbors confirmed that the Israelite God fit this definition. He was the God of gods. The Creator of all. The most fearsome deity who controlled sun, moon, stars, and weather. His gigantic hand had once held back the Red Sea so His people could cross through on dry land. He had created a pillar of fire to lead them by night and a column of cloud to guide them daily. Unlike Rahab, who had to work for her meals, this God had created food from nothing—manna, bread from the ground. He made the arid earth spit up water for His people to drink. He had prevented their shoes from wearing out for forty years. He was powerful, supernatural, and utterly dedicated to the safety of His people. Oh, how she wanted that kind of protection. She begged for it under the silence of the stars.

Footsteps echoed from a stone staircase nearby. Rahab turned toward the noise—two men dressed in traveling clothes, their dialect foreign. A group of local thugs were following close behind them. She heard one say, "What are you doing here, foreigners?"

The men said nothing now, but Rahab saw one of them begin to reach beneath his cloak. Was that a glint of steel she saw in the fading evening light?

She spoke before she thought, spurred only by the instinct to prevent bloodshed. "Oh there you are!" she said, her words confident. "I've been waiting for you both." She eyed the group of men shouting curses behind them. "Never mind you," she told them. "These men are meant to be my guests."

She turned toward home, motioning for the travelers to follow her. "Don't worry," she whispered. "I have enough information on those men to keep them as silent as the night." She said these things to convince herself as well as the strangers, though she knew how loose-lipped that group was. She unlocked her door, shooed the men inside, then barred the inner door. *Who were these men, and what had she just done?*

She asked the men to sit while she gathered what little she had in the kitchen and concocted a small meal.

"Thank you," one of the men said, taking a long drink of well water. "You are to be commended, rescuing us from that mob." There was only the barest trace of irony in his voice. Rahab decided not to mention having seen the knife.

"I cannot explain my actions—only that I knew I needed to help you," she said. That was honest enough.

One of the men cleared his throat. "I am Salmon. This is my companion, Bezai."

"Those are not familiar names." She poured the thirsty men more water from her earthen jug.

"No," Salmon said simply.

Quiet fell between them and lingered as the men ate.

"What is your intent?" Rahab finally asked.

Her guests chewed thoughtfully, but neither offered an answer.

"Please tell me," she finally pressed again. "Why did that group of men follow you?"

"No work of God is without its trials," Salmon said.

"Did you say 'God'? Which one? There are many." With this Rahab let go of decorum. Her place in Jericho's society meant that she did not meet the gaze of men, though they gazed at her aplenty. These men would not be like her faceless clients. No. She needed to know what these men knew—needed to see the sincerity or deception in their eyes.

"We are on a mission from the Almighty," Salmon said. "We are Israelites."

Rahab's throat tightened. She had invited these men into her home. The king had a special regiment spread throughout the city, which meant one thing: if the Israelites were found under her roof, she would be executed. Still, her belief in the power of their God tamped down her panic. Perhaps if she aligned herself with them, all would be well?

Once Salmon's tongue loosed, he spoke freely. He talked of the Israelites' leader, Joshua, their desert wanderings, and the latest feats of the Most High God. "We are spying out this land, your city. We aim to defeat it," he said.

Bezai nodded. "And God is on our side," he said.

Suddenly, a knock shook the outer door. "Rahab! Open up!" a man's voice called.

She prayed to the Israelite God, asking for quick wisdom. "Hurry," she urged her guests in a hushed voice. "The roof." As the pounding at the door continued, she spirited the two men skyward, told them to be as quiet as the dead, then covered them with bundles of flax. Each step down the ladder, she prayed for words to say, protection for her home, and courage.

She opened the door a crack. A messenger of the king of Jericho stood there. Flanking him were several of the king's men. The royal servant's eyes darkened at the sight of her, then settled into lust. She knew that leer all too well. She had seen it a thousand times on the faces of the men who paid her wages. There were few career options for women like Rahab, and she did what she had to in order to survive.

The man crossed his arms across his strong chest and said, "Some Israelites have come here tonight to spy out the land."

"How do you know such a thing?" Rahab kept her voice steady even though her pulse thrummed in her temples.

"A group of men saw them enter your house."

"A lot of men enter my house, sir." She kept the door ajar, not opening it fully. "Besides, isn't that quite a leap to call a traveler a spy? If that's the case, I'm constantly employed by spies." She shook her head. "It's late." She began to shut the door, but the king's messenger wedged his sandal between the door and its jamb.

He leveled a sneer her way. "This is not a request, but a command. Bring out the men who have come into your house, for they have come here to spy out the whole land."

She swatted the air between them. "Yes, the men were here earlier, but I didn't know where they were from." The lie slipped easily from her lips, something she had grown accustomed to in her profession. All was deception when greedy men were involved—it was a necessary evil for survival, though this time the lie thickened her tongue and caused her heart to beat faster. "They left the town at dusk, as the gates were about to close," she continued. "I don't know where they went. If you hurry, you can probably catch up with them."

The men huffed out, leaving only their stench in their wake. She took note of their path—along the road leading to the shallow crossings of the Jordan. As soon as they left, she heard the familiar sound of Jericho's gate slamming shut.

She told herself to breathe. It took some time before her pulse slowed. She mounted the ladder beneath her roof and pulled the flax from the Israelites, exposing their faces to the moonrise.

Salmon thanked her.

"I know the LORD has given you this land," she told them, careful to use the correct name of their all-powerful God.

The two men exchanged glances, eyes wide.

She paced the roof, calculating her words, wanting to say them just so. Her survival depended upon her syntax. "We are all afraid of you. Everyone in the land is living in terror," she finally said.

Rahab sat upon a flax pile on the inner part of her roof and motioned for the men to do the same. She didn't want to risk them being seen, even by an errant child running the pathway around the walled city. "We have heard," she whispered, "how the LORD made a dry path for you through the Red Sea when you left Egypt. And we know what you did to Sihon and Og, the two Amorite kings east of the Jordan River, whose people you completely destroyed."

She, a keen watcher of men, studied their faces to see if their countenances confirmed her words. Both nodded.

The evening breeze loosed a strand of hair, so she tucked it beneath her head covering. "No wonder our hearts have melted in fear! No one has the courage to fight after hearing such things. For the LORD your God is the supreme God of the heavens above and the earth below." It felt good to declare these words aloud to men who would understand. She had caged these very words inside her, afraid to share her burgeoning faith with the people of Jericho whose leadership demanded worship of their gods. She pulled in a new breath, and for the first time felt emancipation from these walls, this situation, her occupation.

She had only one chance for rescue. One moment that would determine her destiny. She beseeched the God of the Israelites for wisdom, for He alone knew what would persuade such men. The idea formed in her mind as quickly as a sandstorm in the desert. She gestured toward the wall, hoping the men would appreciate their own plight. "Now swear to me by the LORD that you will be kind to me and my family since I have helped you." Knowing the Lord by reputation to be One who kept His vows and demanded obedience of those who vowed, she hoped this ploy would work.

Salmon and Bezai nodded at each other. "Go on," Salmon said.

"Give me some guarantee that when Jericho is conquered, you will let me live, along with my father and mother, my brothers and sisters, and all their families." She was careful to name every person in her household because she loved them so. She could not let them suffer harm.

Salmon stood and pointed to himself and Bezai. "We offer our own lives as a guarantee for your safety," he said.

She felt her burden take flight and soar skyward. All of them would be well—as long as they sheltered in her home.

"If you don't betray us, we will keep our promise and be kind to you when the LORD gives us the land," Salmon continued. His eyes could be trusted, and his voice? It did not waver. These were promises etched in stone.

Rahab thanked him, while she internally marveled at his faith. Salmon did not say "*if* the Lord gives us the land," but *when*. She suddenly pitied her fellow Jerichoans, whose misplaced trust in a wall would inevitably become their ruin. If only they could all see what she saw, perceive what she perceived: that when the God of the Israelites came, He would prevail, even against an impenetrable obstacle.

Aware of the fast-approaching dawn, Rahab knew she had to act quickly to rescue these men of the Lord. She grabbed a scarlet linen rope she'd hidden beneath the flax sheaves and motioned for them to follow her to the story below. She secured the rope to an inner doorway, then heaved it over her window ledge. "Escape to the hill country," she told them. "Hide there for three days from the men searching for you. Then, when they have returned, you can go on your way."

The two conferred together in the hallway for a moment. She grew frustrated at their delay, worried the king's men would come soon.

Finally Bezai said, "We will be bound by the oath we have taken only if you follow these instructions."

"Of course." She pointed to the window where the rope of escape hung like a tongue. "But you must hurry."

"When we come into the land," Salmon added, "you must leave this scarlet rope hanging from the window through which you let us down. And all your family members—your father, mother, brothers, and all your relatives—must be here inside the house. If they go out into the street and are killed, it will not be our fault. But if anyone lays a hand on people inside this house, we will accept the responsibility for their death."

Rahab nodded.

In a moment, Salmon and Bezai had scampered down the wall, hit the ground with a thud, and sprinted toward the hill country. With the scarlet rope still lolling from the window, she marveled at what had transpired. Her family would be safe.

Rumors of death spread throughout Jericho. Rahab could feel each person's angst as she hastily bought figs from the market in the city's bowels. A decree of isolation had been delivered by the king. All the doors of their city remained locked, and no one could venture beyond the wall, nor could anyone enter. Every time Rahab returned home, she gazed out the window toward the plains, squinting her eyes to see if any army appeared. For many days, nothing stirred.

But then a puff of dust rose into the halcyon sky in the far distance. "That's them," she told her family. "No one is to leave this house. Do you understand me?" Even her nephews and nieces nodded their assent. They seemed nervous. Perhaps her own twitchiness had infected the entire household.

Rahab watched as the Israelite people slowly made their way toward Jericho. She could hear mustering and battle cries within the city—shouts of war and songs of imminent victory. Her countrymen erred on the side of pride, thinking themselves bigger than the God who created all—even the rocks that made up the wall in which they trusted.

When the nation of Israel marched around her city the first time, she expected a raid immediately, but instead, armed men led the processional, followed by seven men who walked before a golden vessel carried by poles. Each man before the vessel carried a ram's horn, which he blew. Armed men followed, saying nothing as the horns played on. Then the people, children and all, kept their silence as they circumvented their wall.

Still, she looked for Salmon, the taller of the two spies, as the crowd circled. When he walked by, he looked up at her window and nodded as if to say, "Please heed our words, young Rahab."

After they circled the city and blew their horns, the silent Israelites returned to camp. There was no invasion. And no word from Salmon and Bezai. It was most puzzling.

Fear occupied Rahab's mind and heart. Each day, the same pattern emerged—armed men, priestly men, the vessel, armed men, horns blaring, then the people marched without speaking—sparking dread among the citizens of Jericho. Salmon continued to catch her eye each day as he passed below the wall.

Her nephew begged to leave the house to play with his friends in the streets of Jericho. "Please, Aunt Rahab. All these invaders do is march and play music. Surely nothing will come of this."

"Silence," Rahab said. "You must promise me you'll stay safe here with us. If you do not, you will be killed."

Her nephew sulked while the sound of footsteps thumped beyond the wall.

Six days this march went on.

On the seventh, Rahab sensed a change in the air, as if all the world had fallen silent while birds ceased their chirping. No buzzing of bees filled the quiet. The Israelites continued their pattern just as before, only they didn't stop at one time around in their horn processional. No, this time they kept circling. She could feel their footsteps in her heart, sense the vibrations beneath her feet. Something was afoot!

She counted Salmon's route. One. Two. Three. Four. Five. Six...

Suddenly, the man she later learned was Joshua, screamed, "Shout! For the LORD has given you the town! Jericho and everything in it must be completely destroyed as an offering to the LORD." Rahab clutched her chest as he continued, "Only Rahab the prostitute and the others in her house will be spared, for she protected our spies!" she heard him say.

All would be well. She let out a breath as her family huddled nearby.

The man called Joshua continued. "Do not take any of the things set apart for destruction, or you yourselves will be completely destroyed, and you will bring trouble on the camp of Israel. Everything made from silver, gold, bronze, or iron is sacred to the Lord and must be brought into His treasury."

When Joshua ceased speaking, the entire nation below her let out a tremendous shout—equal parts lion, screaming woman, and war cry. Rumbling emerged from beneath her. Then the loud sound of stone striking stone erupted around her. She gathered her family in the safest place she could find—the flax-topped roof—and prayed for safety. Great shouts continued to come from the Israelites as the mighty wall all around her crumbled into immense piles of debris. It was as if the Creator of all things shook the earth just beneath the circumference of the city, rattling it to its foundations. The shouts, the horns, and the terrible rumble of rock falling upon rock, and the cries of her people made Rahab cup her ears and shut her eyes tight.

In the mayhem, Salmon and Bezai found Rahab and her family on the quickly collapsing rooftop and told them to follow closely behind. "We are taking you to a safe place," Salmon said. And that evening, Rahab found herself and her family safe near the camp of Israel.

New beginnings were hard to come by in a closed-off city with closed-off minds. A prostitute would always be a prostitute, no matter how hard she tried to escape her lot. But in this new paradigm, Rahab found a renewed life. No longer known as a prostitute, she now was known by many as a woman whose actions helped bring about a great military victory.

It was Salmon who believed in her kindness first—he whose eyes found hers prior to the deliverance of Jericho. When he looked upon her, lust did not live there, nor gain, but admiration and camaraderie—a shared burden, a celebrated victory. No longer devoid of husband and children, Rahab found herself embraced. Together they would parent Boaz, then grandparent Obed, as the years marched on, much like the Israelites once had around the city of Jericho.

The Biblical Narrative

Prior to Rahab's meeting with the two spies, she had heard about the legendary deeds of the Lord Most High. Hers was a faith that was caught not through experience, but by hearing the stories of things that had taken place far away. The rumors became her reality, and she believed God was a God who protected His people, conquered the Red Sea, and plundered enemy nations before them. Instead of fearing her own king, she feared the King of kings.

Rahab is referred to as a *zonah* three times in the Joshua narrative.[1] The word simply means "prostitute" or "harlot." Josephus categorized her as an innkeeper, as the Hebrew word for prostitute and "female who gives food and provisions" share the same consonants.[2] Still, when she is mentioned later in the biblical text, the authors use the word *prostitute*. Though prostitution was less repugnant in those days than now, it still was not an honorable way to make a living. Rahab's home being situated along the wall meant that many would see her actions and take note of the men who frequented her bed. Even so, we see her exhibiting great compassion toward her family and extended family. There is little indication that they had ostracized her for her profession. During that time period, families usually lived together.

Some scholars believe that Salmon was one of the spies Joshua sent out, but that will be impossible to verify until eternity, when all things are made clear. (I made that speculation in the text.) Salmon was from the tribe of Judah, and after marrying Rahab, later became King David's great-great-grandfather. That makes them both the ancestors of Jesus. Matthew 1:5 tells us, "Salmon was the father of Boaz (whose mother was Rahab). Boaz was the father of Obed (whose mother was Ruth). Obed was the father of Jesse." How powerful Matthew's statements are! Although strictly forbidden to take foreign wives, these Israelite men chose to do so anyway in marrying Rahab and Ruth (who was from Moab). And yet, they are part of the bloodline of Christ! This is further proof that God has always had a heart for the entire world's redemption, not simply the nation of Israel.

Rahab was an Amorite, part of the tradition of idol-worshipping tribes. She must have known about the importance of displaying solidarity with your tribe, but she chose to betray the king of Jericho in order to harbor the Israelite spies. Hers was no simple gamble. If the king found out what she had done, she faced certain execution. This woman immersed in idolatry had an uncanny grasp of the sovereignty of God, and she believed more in His ability to act than any idol's power to overcome His will.

How fitting, then, that Rahab's words echoed Moses and his song of deliverance. After the Red Sea crossing, he had said, "He has hurled both horse and rider into the sea...Pharaoh's chariots and army he has hurled into the sea. The finest of Pharaoh's officers are drowned in the Red Sea. The deep waters gushed over them; they sank to the bottom like a stone" (Exodus 15:1b, 4–5). Rahab told the spies, "For we have heard how the LORD made a dry path for you through the Red Sea when you left Egypt" (Joshua 2:10a). Though she had not been a part of the nation's deliverance, she knew the story well.

The color of the rope hints at past and future salvation as well. Those from the nation of Israel who read this story could not help but remember the Passover where red blood protected them from the Death Angel's sword. "But the blood on your doorposts will serve as a sign, marking the houses where you are staying. When I see the blood, I will pass over you. This plague of death will not touch you when I strike the land of Egypt" (Exodus 12:13). Note that this blood was splashed on the outside of the home, in the same manner as the scarlet rope hung outside Rahab's house as a sign of protection. The people of Jericho could not see the sign, since they were sequestered inside the walls of the city. But the spies could see it clearly. It symbolized Rahab's faith and ensured her safety. Later, the blood of Jesus, shed for us, would become our own scarlet rope of redemption. When God the Father sees those of us who are in Christ, He sees the outward sign of Christ's sacrifice. We are saved because of His blood.

What we most need to remember about Rahab is her faith. She is commended by the writer of Hebrews, as well as James, the Lord's brother. "It was by faith that Rahab the prostitute was not destroyed with the people in her city who refused to obey God. For she had given a friendly welcome to the spies" (Hebrews 11:31). Rahab's hospitality toward the strangers revealed her robust trust in God. Her calm kindness illuminated her belief in God and His promise-keeping abilities. During that era, hospitality meant protecting those within your care, but Rahab exceeded those expectations by risking her life for the two strangers. She is the only woman commended in the list of faith heroes in Hebrews besides Sarah. James writes, "Rahab the prostitute...was shown to be right with God by her actions when she hid those messengers and sent them safely away by a different road" (James 2:25). Rahab reminds us that faith is not merely an inner feeling of confidence—it is a belief backed up by sacrificial action.

In both these passages, Rahab is called a prostitute. This is not meant to be a condemnation, but a testimony to God's power to redeem. Hers is a story of rescue and grace. It's the same reason the woman caught in adultery still has that moniker; it reflects her journey from brokenness to reconciliation and healing. Jesus reminded us when He walked the earth that the Kingdom wasn't prepared for the perfect, but extended toward those who know their need. "Healthy people don't need a doctor—sick people do. I have come to call not those who think they are righteous, but those who know they are sinners and need to repent" (Luke 5:31–32). When Jesus told the Pharisees the parable of the son who says he will obey, then doesn't, followed by the son who says he won't obey, then does, He said, "I tell you the truth, corrupt tax collectors and prostitutes will get into the kingdom of God before you do" (Matthew 21:31).

Rahab demonstrates God's ability to redeem anyone from any circumstance. The story of Rahab is not simply about her bold faith, but a testament to the power of the One in Whom she places her faith.

How This Applies to Misunderstood You

What is compelling about Rahab's story is the two spies' fair-mindedness. Though the text is silent, there's a strong probability the spies knew her occupation. Still, they sheltered with her and did not make any disparaging comments against her. Theirs is an example to all of us who are tempted to define someone solely by their circumstances or their past.

But in the biblical narrative, Rahab never fully sheds her reputation. The label follows her, sticks with her through centuries.

Perhaps you feel that way as well. People are all too quick to remind you of your past shortcomings, often attaching labels to you without permission. Rahab's value was misunderstood. Her social value depended on being used by men for sexual pleasure. In prostitution, most situations are desperate. No little girl dreams of becoming one, but circumstances, exploitation, substance abuse, and unsafe homes have provided fertile ground for prostitution and sex slavery to flourish today. And, unfortunately, the stigma often solely rests upon the woman forced to perform the act. Seldom do the men exploiting them see justice or feel shame. This is a john's world.

This is not new. The woman caught in the very act of adultery in the New Testament is hauled before the religious leaders naked and unaccompanied. Somehow it is deemed to be her fault alone. *The Scarlet Letter* tells the story of Hester Prynne, who must bear the letter of adultery in her community while the man with whom she was sinning stays blissfully unlettered. Women have long been scapegoated for promiscuity while their male counterparts get a pass. The purity movement of the 1990s placed a heavy burden upon girls to be modest so as not to tempt boys, but then failed to address the lust problem boys were expected to have. In short, the onus was on women to make sure men wouldn't lust. Girls in high school who had sex quickly got a reputation, while boys who did the same thing were heralded as virile.

What can a woman who is broken by her sexual past do? So many women have experienced sexual abuse, which led to further promiscuity—but instead of providing solace, shelter, and help, society coldly blames us instead.

The Woman at the Well is instructive for us. She is known as one who had five husbands and one lover. But Jesus simply states the fact without placing shame and blame upon her. Some scholars believe the Samaritan woman may have experienced divorce because she could not provide offspring, which would have allowed a husband to dismiss her with a certificate of divorce. When she admits to her long string of marriages and her current situation (which most likely was the only way she could provide for herself as a barren, unattached woman), Jesus says, "You certainly spoke the truth!" (John 4:18). He does not tell her to repent. He does not call curses down from Heaven upon her. In fact, His discourse with her is the longest theological discussion recorded between Jesus and another human being. We further see His lack of punishment when she tells her village, "Come and see a man who told me everything I ever did! Could he possibly be the Messiah?" (4:29). The result of her joyful proclamation was the village streaming to Jesus (see 4:30).

We need to take away the sting of others' labels, particularly sexual labels. That doesn't mean we abandon sexual ethics or the Bible's very clear words prohibiting sex outside of marriage. But it does mean that we understand all sin, of any type, is leveled at the cross of Christ. All of it, whether gossip or hateful words or lying or sex outside of marriage, hurts our relationship with a holy God. All sin separates, no matter what "type." We seldom see anyone labeled as a "past gossip," but a sexual past follows us the rest of our lives. Just ask Rahab the harlot.

We also forget that Jesus institutes a higher ethic—that our sin does not originate in the body, but in our thought life. When we objectify others, we deny their value. Jesus tells us, "You have heard the commandment that says, 'You must not commit adultery.' But I say, anyone who even looks at a woman with lust has already committed adultery with her in his heart" (Matthew 5:27–28). We are wholly called into sexual purity—cleanness of mind, heart, and body.

So what do we do if we bear the burden of a label? How do we deal with other people's misunderstanding of our state before God? Sadly, we cannot change another's mind. Our reputation cannot be managed perfectly, but we can live lives now of purity and hope. We can take an inventory of our relationships, particularly with those who will not let us move beyond our past labels. (It's important to note that you don't have to wear a sexual label for this to be true. Some women wear labels like "broken," "drug abuser," "anorexic," "bulimic," "divorcee," "mentally ill," or "alcoholic"—to name a few.) If our closest relationships serve to remind us of our past either through taunting, unfair name-calling, or by wooing us back into the lifestyle we have bravely abandoned, we must reevaluate the people with whom we spend our time. The Bible is replete with admonitions about staying away from people who are bad for us. "My child," the author of Proverbs writes, "don't go along with them! Stay far away from their paths. They rush to commit evil deeds. They hurry to commit murder"

(Proverbs 1:15–16). Paul reminds us, "Don't be fooled by those who say such things, for 'bad company corrupts good character'" (1 Corinthians 15:33).

Perhaps our labels feel heavy because others continually remind us of them. Perhaps it's finally time to move on—to create strong boundaries around the bullies in our lives and retrain our minds in the truth.

What is the truth for the child of God?

You are redeemed from a broken past.

You are not the sum of your sins.

You are weighted with worth.

You are set free from the shackles of your childhood.

You are dearly loved by God.

You are welcomed into the family of God.

You are a carrier of light.

You are defined by the character of God.

You are graced with forgiveness.

You are given hope.

You are set free from the law of sin and death.

You are beautiful.

You are worth being protected and cared for.

You have a new purpose.

You are beloved of God.

You are no longer bound to your past.

You are a new creation.

You have been bought with a price.

No matter what your past holds over you, the God of the universe who has sent His Son to die in your place has dealt with your sin. God promises that He forgets our sins precisely because they have been paid for. "And I will forgive their wickedness, and I will never again remember their sins" (Hebrews 8:12). The Gospel is simple, yet profound. Still, we struggle to believe its good news, either because other voices remind us of our past, or because we dredge it up ourselves. The Apostle Paul writes, "He [Christ] canceled the record of the charges against us and took it away by nailing it to the cross" (Colossians 2:14). A few verses later, he reminds the believers not to allow anyone (including yourself) to condemn you. "So don't let anyone condemn you for what you eat or drink, or for not celebrating certain holy days or new moon ceremonies or Sabbaths" (Colossians 2:16).

If you are constantly being misunderstood by those who love you, it's time to remind yourself of the truth of your very real forgiveness. It's time to reevaluate the voices you give power to. It's time to hear the still, small voice of your God, who takes great delight in you. You have been rescued. You stand today clean and set free. Now it's time to shed any moniker of abuse, addiction, neglect, sin, and anguish, choosing instead to walk in freedom. Paul reminds us of this journey of sanctification when he writes, "But that isn't what you learned about Christ. Since you have heard about Jesus and have learned the truth that comes from him, throw off your old sinful nature and your former way of life, which is corrupted by lust and deception. Instead, let the Spirit renew your thoughts and attitudes. Put on your new nature, created to be like God—truly righteous and holy" (Ephesians 4:20–24).

While it is just and right to look on your past, mourn what you find there, and uncover it, there comes a time when you have to stop retrospective living and turn your face toward the future. You are not the sum of your pain; you are being renewed by the God of all creation to do good works—works he prepared beforehand for you to walk into (see Ephesians 2:10). If you allow the words and judgments of others to sideline you, you won't move forward in ministry, life, and health. There are others in your circle of influence who need your forward momentum, people who need rescue and love and hope. Had Rahab allowed her label to inform her actions, she would not have risked her life to save the spies. Hers was an act of betrayal of her own pagan culture and an embrace of the Almighty God who fought on the side of the Israelites. She did not shrink. She did not make excuses for her past. She chose to believe God was bigger than all that, despite her past, and that He would deliver both her and her family.

All that to say, don't let a label prevent you from doing great work, friend.

Truths about Fully Understood You

- No matter what is in your past, God has a unique plan for you.
- Your fidelity to God now matters more than your past decisions.
- When you trust God for what you cannot see, He meets you in that place.
- Old labels don't apply to your new life in Christ.
- God loves to set you free.

Questions for Discussion

1. How did Rahab demonstrate her trust in God when she interacted with the spies?
2. How do you think Rahab learned about the mighty acts of God?
3. Rahab lied to the king's servants in protecting the spies. How do you reconcile her lying with the ultimate good of the nation of Israel? Is it ever OK to lie?
4. In a way, Rahab was enslaved to her town and lifestyle, yet God chose to deliver her and her family. How does

that bring you hope today, particularly if you have an unsaved friend or family member you're praying for?

5. How has God set you free from your past? What do you need to be set free from today?

CHAPTER FIVE

Naomi, the Grieved One

E limelech was a good man who loved his family. When famine struck Bethlehem, he packed up his wife, Naomi, and his two sons, Mahlon and Kilion, leaving the land of Judah for the far country of Moab in hopes of provision and a new life. They found favor there, settling into a home.

Some years later, Elimelech's death took Naomi's breath away. She found him bent over a grinding stone, breathing in raspy heaves. He could not speak, but with his gaze told her he loved her. They held each other's eyes as lovers do in first embrace, but no matter how much she begged God to spare him, willing Elimelech to live, his breaths became sporadic under the Moab sky, and he let the last one clear out. His death deadened her, leaving her alone in a foreign world she never quite adapted to, now bereft of her only companion.

Naomi knew the Law prohibited marriage with pagans, but what could she do? Moab was their home now, and their roots had ten-drilled in deep. They were family—Naomi as matriarch, then Mahlon, Kilion, and their wives Orpah and Ruth.

Naomi tried to pick up the shards of her life, but her mind numbed at the thought of eking out an existence without companionship. Her sons seemed to sense her growing despair and filled small aches in her heart with kind words. Even Orpah and Ruth sensed her grief. Ruth cried alongside her in quiet moments. It was then Ruth held Naomi's hand, comforting her by asking her about her homeland.

Naomi began to see that life could be good, perhaps. Exiled by famine, yes. Widowed, yes. But at least she could look forward to the comfort of grandchildren. Elimelech's line would continue, and life would move on. Hope, a tenuous trait, hung on by a spider's thread. Her two sons shared her lineage; their hearts beat her blood. Yes, she would console herself there.

But ten years after her Elimelech's demise, Mahlon, then Kilion joined their father in death. And every foundation that had once held her fixed crumbled like rocks in an earthquake beneath her feet, leaving her crumpled on the ground, wrung dry of tears.

News came like light poking through the ominous clouds of her depression: God was now blessing her homeland. Crops flourished in Judah. The long famine had ended with newfound prosperity. All her anguish culminated in a longing for home, almost as fierce as her love for Elimelech had been a decade before. She packed her mule, invited Orpah and Ruth to accompany her, and they set out from Moab on the road leading back to Judah.

The dust, the heat, the relentless sun slowed their journey. Naomi took note of the beautiful faces of her daughters-in-law and realized she had been selfish asking them to accompany her. Yes, it would be a dangerous journey toward Bethlehem, but she now was an embittered woman, going home to die. These two young women could have very real futures in their homeland. Who was she to deny them the kind of marriage both she and they had once experienced?

As the sun hit its zenith and they sat beneath a tree to eat flatbread and olives, she mustered up her courage and said, "Go back to your mothers' homes. And may the LORD reward you for your kindness to your husbands and to me. May the LORD bless you with the security of another marriage." *Security,* she thought. *Isn't that what we all long for?* She kissed Orpah, and the tears that had been carefully put away emerged in force. When she said goodbye to Ruth, all three women wept over their lunches.

The girls both argued with Naomi, insisting they wanted to go with her to her people. They wanted to know the world and culture their husbands had come from. Perhaps they felt, thought Naomi, that they would miss her sons less in their native environment.

"Why should you go on with me?" she cried. "Can I still give birth to other sons who could grow up to be your husbands? No, my daughters," she said. "Return to your parents' homes, for I am too old to marry again. And even if it were possible, and I were to get married tonight and bear sons, then what?"

Silence answered back. A mourning dove cooed to fill the quiet.

Naomi took a cloth from her breast and wiped their tears. "Would you wait for them to grow up and refuse to marry someone else? No, of course not, my daughters! Things are far more bitter for me than for you, because the LORD Himself has raised His fist against me."

At this, tears of anger sped down her sun-pinked cheeks. God had forsaken her. She would walk to Judah alone, live off the pity of her people, then return to dust.

Orpah kissed her, bidding her farewell. But Ruth embraced her and would not let her go—the kind of hug that never intended to release its grip. Naomi tried to peel her off, but Ruth clung still. "Look, your sister-in-law has gone back to her people and to her gods. You should do the same."

Ruth broke away, placed her hands on Naomi's shoulders, and held her gaze. "Don't ask me to leave you and turn back," she said. "Wherever you go, I will go; wherever you live, I will live. Your people will be my people, and your God will be my God."

Naomi tried to reason with her determined daughter-in-law, but Ruth would not allow it.

"Wherever you die, I will die, and there I will be buried. May the LORD punish me severely if I allow anything but death to separate us!"

The sun began its descent over the Judean hills. They needed to continue on their journey. Orpah's silhouette faded like a mirage. Naomi picked up her parcel, placed it upon their donkey's shoulders, and walked toward home, Ruth in tow.

Bethlehem rose before them while Naomi fretted. She had left the city as a rich woman with a family—a husband and two strong sons. She now returned in defeat, a Moabitess following behind her. She was the picture of God's neglect, she knew, and she felt the shame rise to warm her cheeks.

At the city gate, her people roused themselves. People buzzed around Naomi and Ruth. She overheard one woman say, "Is it really Naomi?"

"Don't call me Naomi," she responded. "Instead, call me Mara, for the Almighty has made life very bitter for me. I went away full, but the LORD has brought me home empty. Why call me Naomi when the LORD has caused me to suffer and the Almighty has sent such tragedy upon me?"

This quieted the excited crowd. Naomi made her way into the belly of Bethlehem, "the house of bread," as it was known. And as luck would have it, the barley harvest had just begun.

Days seemed dull, the nights duller. Depression tore at Naomi's heart, and she gave into its song of doom. But hunger niggled at her, and she worried she and Ruth would starve. When Ruth volunteered to glean the barley fields, Naomi let her. They might be beggars, but at least they would have grain.

Naomi expected a pittance, perhaps a handful or two. Some farmers had no doubt been trained through years of famine to harvest nearly every last grain, leaving precious few for the poor gleaners. But when Ruth returned with an entire basketful, she marveled. "Where did you gather all this grain today? Where did you work? May the LORD bless the one who helped you!"

"The man I worked with today is named Boaz," Ruth said.

Her words were simple enough, but to Naomi, they were weighted with possibility.

Naomi stood, and in the standing felt a bit of her weariness fall away. "May the LORD bless him! He is showing his kindness to us as well as to your dead husband. That man is one of our closest relatives, one of our family redeemers." She then explained to Ruth what that meant—that Boaz could rescue them all, including their future lineage.

Ruth hugged Naomi. "What's more," she said, eyes shining as she released her, "Boaz even told me to come back and stay with his harvesters until the entire harvest is completed."

Naomi bustled around their small home. She couldn't think standing still, so she puttered around making room for their abundant barley harvest. "Good," she finally said. "Do as he said, my daughter. Stay with his young women right through the whole harvest. You might be harassed in other fields, but you'll be safe with him."

Ruth, with her kind eyes and benevolent heart, obeyed Naomi's directive. Through the spring she harvested barley, and in the early summer she harvested wheat.

"My daughter," Naomi said to Ruth, fresh from gleaning. "It's time that I found a permanent home for you, so that you will be provided for."

"But—" Ruth protested.

Naomi shushed her as they sat near the dusky opening of their cottage's window. "Boaz is a close relative of ours, and he's been very kind by letting you gather grain with his young women." Naomi stood and paced the dust floor. "Now do as I tell you—take a bath and put on perfume and dress in your nicest clothes." She pointed out the doorway. "Then go to the threshing floor, but don't let Boaz see you until he has finished eating and drinking." She returned to Ruth and bent near her daughter-in-law, quieting her voice. "Be sure to notice where he lies down; then go and uncover his feet and lie down there. He will tell you what to do."

Ruth's face reddened at Naomi's suggestion. For a long moment, Ruth kept silent as the day turned to night. She sighed, cupped Naomi's face in her young hands, and smiled. "I will do everything you say." She left that evening as Naomi's prayers followed her through the doorway.

After a toss-and-turn night, Naomi watched from the window, wondering what had transpired.

Ruth returned at dawn, carrying her cloak filled with barley.

"What happened, my daughter?" Naomi asked.

Ruth recounted her time at the feet of Boaz, how he startled awake to her asking him to cover her as the family redeemer. "He blessed me, Naomi," she said, eyes bright. "He praised my loyalty and virtue. He told me not to worry, that he would take care of everything at Bethlehem's gate."

Naomi clasped her hands together. For the first time in a season, she felt hope. The Almighty had not completely forsaken her! Boaz could be the kinsman redeemer they needed—a relative whose purchase of their ancestral land would mean Ruth would now share in the inheritance that was once Naomi's through her husband. All would be well.

"There is one problem," Ruth said. "There is another family redeemer who is more closely related than Boaz. He said if that man will not redeem me, he will do it himself!"

Naomi clapped her hands together. She took note of Ruth's hesitation, the slight fear in her eyes. "Just be patient, my daughter, until we hear what happens. The man won't rest until he has settled things today."

News came in spurts that day. First the other family redeemer said he would do his duty and purchase the land, securing both Ruth and Naomi's future. Then he said he wouldn't do it. Then the redeemer removed his sandal as a signal that he relinquished his right to the property (and the women), and told Boaz, "You buy the land."

Boaz then addressed all the people, calling them witnesses to his purchase of Naomi's property—that of her husband and her sons. In that, he took Ruth as his wife—taking her from destitution to delight. A son would come, Lord willing, furthering the line of Elimelech.

The blessing came swift as an eagle. "May the LORD make this woman who is coming into your home like Rachel and Leah, from whom all the nation of Israel descended! May you prosper in Ephrathah and be famous in Bethlehem. And may the LORD give you descendants by this young woman who will be like those of our ancestor Perez, the son of Tamar and Judah." These words felt like melody to Naomi. Where she had existed in shades of gray, accompanied by a dirge, her heart now sang like a trilling bird.

Ruth became the wife of Boaz, and the blessing of God brought baby Obed to Naomi's empty heart. The women who had greeted her at the gate in her disgrace now laughed and delighted. "Praise the LORD, who has now provided a redeemer for your family! May this child be famous in Israel," they proclaimed. Naomi treasured every word, tried to remember the tenor and the form of them so she could recite the blessings again and again. She knew how quickly life could shift, and she needed these words as reminders of God's goodness. "May he restore your youth and care for you in your old age," the women sang. "For he is the son of your daughter-in-law who loves you and has been better to you than seven sons!"

Naomi looked over at Ruth, who beamed under the sun's gaze. Ruth took baby Obed, carefully swaddled, and placed him in Naomi's arms. She gazed down upon his starlit eyes, the smallest of noses, and pinked lips, and fell in love with him. She pulled him close to her, inhaling his new scent. A neighbor bent low and touched Obed's forehead. "Now at last Naomi has a son again!" she said.

And it was true.

The Biblical Narrative

The book of Ruth was written during the era of Judges. During this time in Israel's history, the nation seesawed between blessing and curses, based on its obedience and idolatrous disobedience. Naomi's story mirrors the desolation and restoration process known in that time before Israel had a king. Read that way, we see many parallels to the trials and brokenness of the nation. Even in utter barrenness, where all hope is lost and bitterness abounds, God has compassion on Israel, and ultimately on humanity as He sends Jesus as our Kinsman Redeemer. Naomi's story, then, becomes our salvation story, delineating our lives before Christ (bitter, hard, broken) and our lives after Christ (blessed, abundant, hopeful).

Naomi's name is instructive. It means "pleasantness," "beautiful," "gentle," and "agreeable." But partway through the narrative, she renames herself *Mara*, a name that means "bitterness" or "the sea is bitter." Her new name is an expression of grief. The former Naomi, full of promise and pleasantness, is replaced by an embittered, grieving widow. Renaming oneself is a rare occurrence in the Bible. Usually someone else renames you, so for Naomi to instigate this change reveals the level of her desperation. In her grief, though, she cannot see what she really has. She says she has and is nothing, but she still possesses the loyal love of her daughter-in-law, Ruth. She has her faculties. And, in Bethlehem, she still has extended family. Sometimes grief prevents us from seeing what is good.

Elimelech means "God is my king," and yet in his death, all seems lost. *Mahlon* and *Kilion* mean "sickness" and "used up," respectively. This may hint at the reasons for their deaths. *Orpah* means "back of the neck," as she turned her back on Naomi. *Ruth* means "lovely friend." She is a companion who sticks closer than kin—she chose to remain by Naomi's side though she was not bound to. *Boaz* means "powerful" or "strong." He is the kind of man who could redeem such a desperate situation.

The structure of the book of Ruth is itself a chiasm—an ancient storytelling technique that looks like the tip of an arrow when mapped out. What we begin with, we end with. Every detriment in the first part of the book is met with a fulfillment at the end. The tip of the arrow, then, is the culmination of the story. In modern storytelling we have an inciting incident, conflicts and a rising action, then a climax followed by a denouement—a resolution. So the arrow point of modern stories is seen about 90 percent of the way through. In a chiasm, the arrow point is the central part of the story, firmly fixed in the middle.

The overall chiastic structure of this tale starts with the family of Elimelech in Bethlehem, followed by the story of the women of that family and their husbands' demise in Moab. Next comes a trek to Bethlehem, where Ruth gleans Boaz's barley field. This culminates in the threshing-floor scene where she dramatically places herself at Boaz's feet. Then Boaz buys back what was lost, and the book finishes with the beginning of a new family.

We begin with a fully intact family. We see the disaster of that family, then its restoration. The centrality of the book and its message fall in the scene of Boaz's choice to redeem a widow.

The story opens with famine—ironic, since *Bethlehem* means "house of bread." Famine reduces this breadbasket to barrenness. Naomi experiences a reverse exodus: she leaves Bethlehem full, but in Moab she becomes empty. She exits a wife and mother, but becomes a widow and a childless woman.

Where Elimelech and Naomi chose to go indicates the level of idolatry in Israel at the time. They didn't merely travel to nowhere to hide out and rebuild a life; they relocated to Moab—a known enemy of Israel and a hotbed of idolatry.

The origins of Moab are highlighted in Genesis 19:30–38, when Lot's daughters took turns sleeping with their father because they had no husbands. When the oldest gave birth, she named her son Moab. His children became the nation of the Moabites, occupying land near modern-day Jordan directly east of the Dead Sea. The word *Moab* means "from the father," indicating the family's incestuous roots. The nation was at odds with Israel for centuries; early in Israel's history, the army defeated kings Og and Sihon in the land of Moab. King Balak of Moab attempted to thwart and curse the Israelites by employing the prophet Balaam, who was then halted by a talking donkey. It was in the plains of Moab that Moses peacefully transferred his leadership to Joshua. Israel experienced eighteen years of oppression under King Eglon of Moab. Later, Ehud delivered them (see Judges 3:12–31). Later, another war was waged on Moab's plains (see 2 Kings 3). The psalmist decries Moab, writing, "But Moab, my washbasin, will become my servant, and I will wipe my feet on Edom and shout in triumph over Philistia" (Psalm 60:8). Two prophets recount Moab as the enemy of Israel (see Isaiah 15–16 and Jeremiah 48).

The word "empty" is used twice in the narrative when Naomi describes herself after all her losses. She is barren of love and womb. The writer uses it again when Boaz tells Ruth to take six scoops of barley back to her mother-in-law in Chapter Three. "Don't go back to your mother-in-law *empty*-handed," he says. Here again we see the brilliant literary device of chiasm at work: what was emptied has now been filled.

Naomi uses the word *sons* in Ruth 1:5. The word is best translated "kids" or "lads." It's the only time the word is used in the Old Testament to refer to grown men. Later, the writer of Ruth uses the same idiomatic word to describe Obed, the child who would change Naomi's barrenness to abundance. God took away her kids, then replaced them with this son of promise.

There's also a repetition of the word *wings*. Boaz says this to Ruth: "May the LORD, the God of Israel, under whose wings you have come to take refuge, reward you fully for what you have done" (2:12). Ruth uses the same word when she asks Boaz to spread his *covering* over her. He has the potential to be Ruth's refuge through marriage; he becomes the wings that cover her.

It's also important to note that Naomi calls Ruth "my daughter" throughout the narrative, though she is the daughter of a Moabite woman. When Naomi implores both Orpah and Ruth to return to their own mothers, she calls down *hesed* upon them (God's loyal, covenant-keeping love). Though others refer to Ruth as Naomi's daughter-in-law, her affection marks her firmly as a daughter. She turns out to be better than even Naomi's sons, which the women of her village proclaim. "For he is the son of your daughter-in-law who loves you and has been better to you than seven sons" (Ruth 4:15).

One could study the book of Ruth and mine its intricacies for years, particularly in considering it as a signpost of what Jesus would do through His sinless life, sacrificial death, and beautiful resurrection. He, indeed, is our Kinsman Redeemer, rescuing the outcast and foreigner and providing a new family and heritage. We've had moments when we felt like Mara, but now we cry *Maranatha*, "Come, Lord Jesus." We once had no hope in the world, no prospects beyond what we could scratch out for ourselves, but now we've been graced with a clean slate, a new hope, and a holy task. While we were sinners, Christ died for us (see Romans 5:8). And now we're welcomed into the family of God.

How This Applies to Misunderstood You

As I think about Naomi, I can't help but ponder her self-naming. *Mara*. It has the same root as my own name, and I've struggled for years with it. Am I bitter? Am I broken beyond repair? Have I lost hope? Yes, many times. Often. Grief has tentacles that reach into every aspect of my life. Have you experienced that too?

How is Naomi misunderstood? The scene of her routine reminds us of how difficult it is to live after grief strikes. At the end of Ruth 1, the women of Bethlehem are thrilled to celebrate Naomi's return. But she will have none of their festivities. She shuts down the revelry by invoking that bitter name. The townspeople expected excitement; they got bereavement. Thankfully, the chapter ends with a promise of hope: the beginning of the barley harvest.

Hope is an important place to rest in the midst of grief. For the child of God, there is always hope. There is always another turn in the story, a place where God works even when our emotions tell us He works for other people but not for us. Our grief and depression cloud our vision, removing the color of life and painting it in shades of gray and black. And yet...the barley harvest is nigh.

But I'm getting ahead of myself.

The townspeople expected joy, but they got deep grief. They misunderstood Naomi, expecting her to rejoice as her feet touched Bethlehem's threshold. But she did not. And many of us have experienced the same problem. When we are living in the aftermath of death, trauma, injury, or relational angst, we exist in a state of grief. So often the church cannot handle such sadness. People within the church are often okay with grief—but only for a season. It's like there's a prescribed period of time (and it is brief) that we are allowed sadness, and then it's time to dust ourselves off, push the pain down, and pretend nothing is wrong.

Problem is, pain and grief linger if they're not addressed. This is precisely why so many of the Psalms follow the pattern of lament. They give us a pathway to process our pain in a productive, honest way. Sadly, though, many people don't like to listen to our laments over the long term. Many misunderstand the longevity of trauma and its after-effects. It's inconvenient to walk a friend through the quagmire of grief;

it takes sacrifice, patience, and godliness—qualities sorely lacking in today's evangelical landscape.

When we are misunderstood in our grief, it's a double wound. Not only do we continue to have the existing grief, but we also have to navigate the unrealistic expectations of another. No one has permission to prescribe your recovery journey or how long it will take. That's between you and the Lord. To be rushed through it by an impatient friend or family member demonstrates a deep level of misunderstanding.

Grief is lonely. The descendants of Korah knew it well:

> Can those in the grave declare your unfailing love?
> Can they proclaim your faithfulness in the place of destruction?
> Can the darkness speak of your wonderful deeds?
> Can anyone in the land of forgetfulness talk about your righteousness?
> O Lord, I cry out to you.
> I will keep on pleading day by day.
> O Lord, why do you reject me?
> Why do you turn your face from me?
> I have been sick and close to death since my youth.
> I stand helpless and desperate before your terrors.
> Your fierce anger has overwhelmed me.
> Your terrors have paralyzed me.
> They swirl around me like floodwaters all day long.
> They have engulfed me completely.
> You have taken away my companions and loved ones.
> Darkness is my closest friend. (Psalm 88:11–18)

The way through this kind of misunderstanding is twofold: petition and education.

Petition

The Psalmist talked to God about his sadness. He told the truth about it, directing his anger, bewilderment, and grief Godward. Perhaps he felt God misunderstood his predicament. (Although we know that God knows all, our valid emotions sometimes cause us to question God's understanding of our situation.) That's the beauty of lament: when you're feeling misunderstood in your grief, you can find solace in knowing you are not new to this journey. Grief is an ancient struggle. But how can you follow in the footsteps of those who lamented well?

First, read several lament psalms (3, 6, 7, 13, 30, 34, 43, 44, 51, 59, 60, 74, 79, 88, 102, 137). Then take note of their helpful structure:

1. A complaint about a painful situation, or questions about why God doesn't seem to be helping in grief
2. A request that God would act on the psalmist's behalf
3. A confession of trust in God despite his current struggle
4. An offer to praise God in the midst of the pain
5. An assurance that God is in control

Next, take pen to paper and write out your own lament. Processed pain has a chance to heal, but unprocessed pain festers inside you, eventually erupting in unwanted words or behavior, causing further opportunities for misunderstanding. Give full vent to your stress, worry, angst, and pain. Let God know you're furious. (He already knows you are.) That's why prayer is so powerfully healing—because you are simply interacting with God about what is already known and true. Remember, the Lord has big shoulders, and He can carry every one of your griefs. He is not shocked by your anger or taken aback by your complaints. While others may misunderstand you, God does not. After all, He sent His Son to experience the heartache of Earth. He is the great empathetic savior.

So then, since we have a great High Priest who has entered heaven, Jesus the Son of God, let us hold firmly to what we believe. This High Priest of ours understands our weaknesses, for he faced all of the same testings we do, yet he did not sin. So let us come boldly to the throne of our gracious God. There we will receive his mercy, and we will find grace to help us when we need it most. (Hebrews 4:14–16)

Follow the lament structure above. Complain. Ask God to intervene. Confess your tentative trust. Praise Him in the midst of your pain. Remind yourself that God remains in control. I have had the privilege of leading many through this exercise. It's amazing to me how much it has helped to voice or write out our anger to the One who already knows what's in our hearts. This practice does not heal you, but it inaugurates the healing journey. Naomi's naming herself *Mara* was part of her lament. "The Almighty has made life very bitter for me. I went away full, but the LORD has brought me home empty. Why call me Naomi when the LORD has caused me to suffer and the Almighty has sent such tragedy upon me?" (Ruth 1:20–21).

You see a similar pattern in the book of Job, where the righteous man loses nearly everything. He writes,

> Oh, why give light to those in misery,
> and life to those who are bitter?
> They long for death, and it won't come.
> They search for death more eagerly than for hidden treasure.
> They're filled with joy when they finally die,
> and rejoice when they find the grave.
> Why is life given to those with no future,
> those God has surrounded with difficulties?

I cannot eat for sighing;
my groans pour out like water.
What I always feared has happened to me.
What I dreaded has come true.
I have no peace, no quietness.
I have no rest; only trouble comes. (3:20–26)

It's interesting to note that Job writes his lament in poetry. Sometimes prose is not enough to express the anguish of one's soul. In those deeper spaces of pain, only poetry provides the proper container for lament.

Lamenting moves you through grief toward healing, though the process is neither easy nor linear. It's your first step toward the healing journey, and it's an important one.

Education

While it seems unfair to have to educate people about our grief (why can't they just understand our heart?), sometimes it's necessary to clear up a misunderstanding. When someone levels a cliché our way like, "Why can't you just move on?" we can either retreat and lick obvious wounds, or we can petition God, then educate our friend with kindness. Sadly, we've lost this disciplined art through a lack of face-to-face interaction. We avoid conflict in person and instead level accusations in callous ways over social media. This disconnected practice has emaciated our ability to "speak the truth in love, growing in every way more and more like Christ, who is the head of his body, the church" (Ephesians 4:15).

How will we clear up misunderstandings if we don't talk things out? How will we find new levels of understanding and conciliation if we don't address the elephants (and tigers and buffalos) in our midst? When we are asked to rush grief, it's imperative that we let folks know that grief is a longstanding "gift" that keeps on giving. Letting people into our emotional landscape helps them understand our pain and current struggles.

It's important to note that there are people to whom we should not entrust our heart. Some of these unsafe people will take our pearls of pain and trample them underfoot. Fools, says the book of Proverbs, are all around us, and they are not good guardians of our hearts. The difficult task, though, is knowing who is unsafe and who is safe. Proverbs 26:24–26 cautions, "People may cover their hatred with pleasant words, but they're deceiving you. They pretend to be kind but don't believe them. Their hearts are full of many evils. While their hatred may be concealed by trickery, their wrongdoing will be exposed in public."

One way to determine this is to test your story with a friend or family member and see how they respond. If you try to explain your current pain and are dismissed, chided, demeaned, disbelieved, or discredited, it may be an indication that the person is unsafe. No matter how much you try to explain your grief, they will choose not to understand. In that case, you have a proactive choice to make: live with the reality of being misunderstood, or take your pain elsewhere.

Sometimes there is no way of convincing someone of the truth of your journey. Sometimes their choice to misunderstand your heart is set in stone, immovable, no matter how many educated words you toss their way in kindness.

By speaking the truth to someone who misunderstands you, you're actually offering the gift of growth. You're giving that person the opportunity to "be happy with those who are happy, and weep with those who weep" (Romans 12:15). But if they choose not to weep with you, there's nothing you can do, except not retaliate. "Never pay back evil with more evil. Do things in such a way that everyone can see you are honorable," the Apostle Paul writes in Romans 12:17. The next verse is a beautiful dose of reality: "Do all that you can to live in peace with everyone" (Romans 12:18). The ESV uses this phraseology: "So far as it depends on you, live peaceably with all." You cannot force reconciliation. You can only foster an environment where reconciliation could happen. Express yourself in love. Measure their response. If it's unkind or delves into further misunderstanding, move on, knowing you did what you could to remedy the misunderstanding.

This is why lament is so powerful. No matter how people misunderstand you, you always have the opportunity to tell the Lord how you're feeling. You always have an open channel of communication with God, who understands what it's like to be misunderstood, maligned, and betrayed. Even if 100 percent of the people in your life leave you and hurt you (oh, I hope that never happens), you still have a friend in Jesus. He will carry your grief. "He was despised and rejected—a man of sorrow, acquainted with deepest grief. We turned our backs on him and looked the other way. He was despised, and we did not care" (Isaiah 53:3).

Even though we have forsaken Jesus, He has not forsaken us. In this prophecy of the coming Messiah, which Jesus reads in a synagogue when He begins His earthly ministry, we are reminded of the tender compassion of a God who sees us. "Yet it was our weaknesses he carried; it was our sorrows that weighed him down" (Isaiah 53:4). Jesus carries our brokenness even today. Not only that, He carries *us*. Where we are. How we are. As we are. "He was beaten so we could be whole. He was whipped so we could be healed" (Isaiah 53:5b). He endured all that pain so he could empathize with, help, and carry us. That is the God we serve—a compassionate God, full of loyal love.

Truths about Fully Understood You

- No matter how deep your grief, God's care is deeper still.
- Though you will walk through broken, bitter times, God is working behind the scenes for your good.
- Heartache cannot undermine God's will for you.

- God brings life, even when your dream seems dead.
- God loves to bring faithful, caring people into your life.

Questions for Discussion

1. In seeing the chiastic structure of the book of Ruth, we see the culmination of the story at the threshing floor. Why is this the central, most important part of the story?

2. How does Ruth demonstrate loyal love (*hesed*) to Naomi? Who has been a Ruth in your life? When have you been a Ruth in someone else's life?

3. How does Boaz represent a type of Christ in this story? How has Jesus redeemed you? What has he set you free from?

4. Does anything bother you about this story? How would you have rewritten it? Have you experienced a tragedy that you'd love to see either erased or reversed?

5. You see the missionary heart of God in this story, pursuing those who were not a part of Israel (in the Moabite Ruth). How does that encourage you to reach out to those outside your circle?

CHAPTER SIX

Bathsheba, the Harmed One

Bathsheba lived under the beautiful weight of her name. As the seventh daughter of Eliam, her name had two meanings: "the seventh daughter" and "the daughter of an oath." She often wondered what that meant for her, seven being the number of holy completion and an oath being a strong bond of allegiance. She'd long heard the stories of her father, whose name meant "God is gracious," and his exploits as one of King David's royal officers. It was through this connection that Eliam betrothed her to one of David's mighty men—Uriah.

She made her oath to the Almighty that she would love Uriah the rest of her life. And he reciprocated in kind, but with an addition on their wedding day. "You are the Rose of Sharon," he said. "A beautiful bride. You are God's great gift to me." His was a hungry dedication. He never ceased to remind her of the beauty he saw in her eyes. And under kindness like that, her beauty flourished. That's what love did.

Her husband carried great weight in David's army as a commander of one of its thirty regiments. Though a Hittite and a foreigner, Uriah had spent his life in strength, honor, and duty. Though his heritage followed him, Uriah chose to become an Israelite, heroic and wholly dedicated to the cause of Yahweh. This, Bathsheba loved—not only his exploits, but his heart. Theirs was a convivial relationship of laughter and connection, envied by many whose marriages were more institutional than romantic. Uriah spent his days at home singing to her, regaling her with epic stories of soldiers, the lands they conquered, and the wilds of the outer edges of King David's kingdom. He was at his best when he told stories, and she coaxed them out of him whenever she could.

What did she long for? A child—a son with Uriah's valor and her tenderness, with bright eyes, strong arms, and a love for the Almighty. But month after month, her womb remained barren, and she ached at the thought. So many *mikvehs* she spent praying, hoping that this time her monthly cycle would cease. The only time resentment crept into her heart was when Uriah's exploits prevented him from returning home, lessening their chances of having a family. When he did cross the threshold of their home, she wrapped herself around him, holding onto hope and love and completion.

But the completion remained incomplete.

Bathsheba sank into melancholy the moment Uriah left home to battle Israel's enemies. As he did, she battled her own. She prayed. She lamented. She fasted. She feasted. She lay flat on the cold tile of her bedchamber, begging God to please see her and open her womb, for Heaven's sake. But the heavens remained mute.

The scent of spring reignited her desire for Uriah, his presence, his child—at least that was the hope she cradled to her chest. Another campaign against the Ammonites left her bereft and lonely. Despondent.

That morning brought mourning as her monthly flow finished, reminding her of her barrenness and her need for cleansing. There would be no child this month. Only uncleanness and longing.

As the sunshine warmed her, she made her way to the rooftop to bathe away her grief and impurity in peace. She let out the breath she had been holding in all morning as the sun warmed her face. Perhaps all would be well, she thought. She considered how the light of spring was turning everything verdant on the hills of Judea as she stepped into the *mikveh*. With deliberateness, she poured water over herself, asking God to please cleanse her from bitterness and the gnawing ache of loneliness. Each shower of water became a small hint of emancipation to her. Soon, she would be clean. Soon, Uriah would arrive home and lie with her. Perhaps his child would soon kick within her womb.

Her soul felt alive like it had not in a very long time.

Bathsheba pulled her wrappings around herself and shivered as she picked her way down the stairs into her home below, cleansed from her ritual impurity. She covered her now-wet hair and put on her evening clothes.

Suddenly an insistent knock interrupted her quiet regathering. A servant approached her as she finished dressing. "Several of the king's men are outside. They said they must speak to you at once."

The bottom fell out of her heart. *No. Not Uriah. It cannot be.* Never had she been visited by the king's men before now. Their presence meant only dire news.

As Bathsheba made her way toward the door, she wanted to pace slowly, delaying the inevitable grief. But she could not walk a snail's pace for long.

Several men stood in the fading light. One came to the front of the group, his hands clasped together in front of him. He would not meet her eyes, though she tried to catch his to ascertain the tenor of the news he brought.

"You are Bathsheba, daughter of Eliam, wife of Uriah?"

"It is as you say." She swallowed.

"The king has need of you," he said.

"What is the news of Uriah? Surely you can tell me here." Her heart thrummed a drumbeat beneath her ribcage. Her stomach soured.

But the man said nothing. Instead, he grabbed her elbow with force and began "walking" her toward the palace. Bathsheba looked back at her servant whose face only showed fear and disbelief. What was this about?

"I don't understand," she said.

The other men surrounded her as the first continued to force her forward. Their faces were like stone, nothing more. They said nothing. Instead, they marched her to the palace entrance.

"Why am I being summoned?" she asked.

Nothing.

The heavy door opened to a wide portico where the king's officials milled around. None stole a glance her way. It was as if she were a ghost making her way through the hallway, surrounded and yet unseen. Her feet quietly slapped the ornate tile beneath them with every step. "Where are you taking me?" she managed to ask.

But again, silence.

They mounted the stairs and circled around to the living quarters of the palace, well into its bowels. She wanted to ask more questions, but she now understood the futility. Perhaps the king's respect for Uriah meant he would tell Bathsheba of his demise himself. Certainly, with his dedication and valor, this made sense.

The men opened a giant double door. It creaked upon its hinges. Inside stood the king, but he was not wearing the robes he wore for state business. He looked ordinary somehow, more like a man than a king.

"Leave her," he commanded his servants.

There she stood, hair still wet beneath her head covering, shivering though not cold. Now the news would be delivered, and she would fall to the floor in grief.

She took in four steady breaths as the king said nothing to her, his eyes scanning her body, then meeting her eyes.

Waiting for him to speak, she swallowed.

But he said nothing of Uriah.

Instead, he performed the act reserved only for Uriah as if it were his right—leaving her shaking and broken.

The same men who had forced her to the palace walked her back home. She stumbled as they pushed her forward through the threshold, and a single tear fell down her cheek. She ran past her servant, up the stairs, and collapsed into sobs in her bedchamber until her tears ran dry. Though intrinsically she knew she had no choice in what David had done—she would never have chosen *that!*—guilt still strangled her. What would dear Uriah think of her? She curled in on herself, feeling the sting of her injuries, begging God to kill her. But God's answer was silence.

"I am pregnant."

Three words that were supposed to be a joyful proclamation to her beloved now echoed through her chamber like a death sentence. Uriah had spent all his time since that brutal day in a fierce campaign, not returning home to reseal their love. He would soon know of her secret. *God Almighty, do You even see me?*

She sent for a messenger, then handed him a tightly bound scroll with the three indicting words hidden within it. "This is for the king only. Be sure he receives it," she told the young man.

Later, Bathsheba learned of David's conniving, how he had ushered Uriah home, hoping he would sleep with her to cover up the king's actions. But she knew the honor of her husband. In the midst of war, he was a soldier solely, and he lived his loyalty with passion. He would not darken their doorstep, wouldn't so much as glance her way, until he was officially free of his duties. Odd that his loyalty to the king would put him in danger from the very one he served. When Uriah returned again to the field of war without returning to her, Bathsheba's stomach emptied and emptied. She wept as it happened, marking the unfairness of life. A child should be welcomed, not dreaded. Bathsheba could not tell the difference between sickness from pregnancy and her lovesick fear for Uriah. Messengers from the palace relayed David's mania of late, how he stalked the corridors, muttered to himself, and kept calling for Joab, who led the war effort David had chosen to stay home from.

"He has written a letter to Joab," one of Bathsheba's informants at the palace told her.

"This will not end well," she told her servant girl, then promptly threw up again as a knock sounded below. She wiped her mouth, then greeted a messenger who stood stock-still in her doorway.

"Uriah is dead," the messenger told her.

Three more damning words that she could not control, could not alter. What could a woman do? What could a subject of a king who would do such things do to escape the inevitable? She pulled a black veil over herself like a shroud. Upon her bed, she wanted to lie flat on her stomach, but the insistent kicks of the little one growing there kept her on her side. Tears wound down her cheeks, over the ridge of her nose, into the bedding. Here she remained for many days, refusing food. She wished her bed would swallow her so she could sleep with Uriah in the afterlife. There, they could be together. There, she would be comforted. There, she would be delivered from this impossible predicament.

Death did not come. Instead, life continued to kick its way into her heart. No matter what she dreaded about what lay ahead, no matter how she grieved her beloved's loss, no matter how she became pregnant at the hands of a hungry madman, one thing was true: she would be a mother—a longing fulfilled. But the fulfillment was bittersweet.

Murmurings from the palace filled her with dread. The king, it was said, was making arrangements for another bride to come into his fold. Bathsheba knew she herself was the woman they whispered of. She bit her cheek until it bled, pounded fists against the rock wall of her home, and paced endlessly. But no matter how she protested, no matter how much grief and bewilderment assaulted her, the inevitability haunted her. She would be the wife of a murderer. She would have to sleep with the man who had killed her husband and stolen her innocence.

Her stomach continued its revolt. She lost weight instead of gaining it. Her cheeks became as hollow as her soul. When David's men came for her, she acquiesced, but her heart was dead. The only thing keeping her alive was the steady kick of her unborn child.

When her darling baby yelped into the world, Bathsheba felt both elation and dread. This baby was the result of an unholy union, but she loved him fiercely. She could not bring herself to name the child, and she stole every last moment with him, noting his pink face, the blueness of his eyes, his peaceful slumber. She did not allow a wet nurse to feed him, cherishing his need. She loved providing him nourishment. It was as if each feeding, though it drained her of milk, fed her soul, kept her alive.

The day Nathan the prophet approached the king, Bathsheba fretted. Surely a prophet of the Most High God knew the secret of this baby's origins. She waited quietly around the corner from the throne room, hoping not to be noticed while the baby slept in her arms. When Nathan told David the story of the poor man who loved his little lamb, and the rich man who had stolen and killed it, tears came again. Bathsheba felt her widowhood in her gut and missed Uriah even more. Theirs had been a comfortable, sweet, and joyful union. Not a moment went by where she didn't pine for his embrace, his scent, that look he gave her when he saw her upon his return from battle. King David had stolen all that from her—but not only that, he had robbed her of even saying one last goodbye.

When Nathan declared, "You are that man!" he did so with vigor. His baritone voice reverberated throughout the palace. Bathsheba looked around, wondering how everyone would respond to such a public accusation. He called Bathsheba "Uriah's wife," which was a statement of cruel truth. She had belonged to Uriah. Now she was living a stolen life.

Bathsheba traced her son's cheek as her tears dropped onto his forehead.

"I have sinned against the Lord," she heard David say. Tears followed. Then terrible consequences.

Nathan said a lot of things, but all she could hear was, "Your child will die."

Three words. *I am pregnant.*

Three words. *Uriah is dead.*

Four words. *Your child will die.*

All shuttered her heart. She returned to her chamber, nursed the unnamed boy, and wept afresh. How much longer would she hold this child in her arms?

Seven days was God's answer. The boy's pink face turned ashen as he attempted to inhale, but wheezed instead. His arms went limp. His sky-blue eyes clouded. When he breathed his last, Bathsheba held him to her chest, rocking him, longing for his cry. She would bury him in the City of David just outside the palace grounds.

When David returned from the Tabernacle, he entered her chamber. Eyes wet from grief, he reached out to her, but she did not return his embrace. Her arms felt limp at her side, and she willed her heart to stop beating. David held onto her fiercely and said nothing. The baby that once connected them made no cry, but in the echoing room, David's sobs erupted, igniting her own. Theirs was a shared grief, though not a shared guilt. He comforted her, then, and she once again consummated the union at his request.

When Solomon made his entrance into the world, Nathan brought word that his name should be *Jedidiah*, "beloved of the Lord." All Bathsheba knew was this: her son would be great, and he would bring peace, perhaps even to her. He would be Solomon, the boy of peace.

The Biblical Narrative

Nowhere does the Bible condemn Bathsheba for David's sin. Nathan does not confront her and say, "You are that woman." And God holds David to account, not Bathsheba. We have to understand the dynamics of a kingdom, not glancing our Western eyes toward the text. When a king summoned a subject, there was little one could do about it. David was sovereign over Israel, and what he demanded he got. You can see this type of kingly dynamic in the book of Esther when she says, "All the king's officials and even the people in the provinces know that anyone who appears before the king in his inner court without being invited is doomed to die unless the king holds out his gold scepter. And the king has not called for me to come to him for thirty days" (Esther 4:11). The king wielded ultimate power, including the power of death.

Bathsheba's bathing has been scrutinized and misunderstood by many. In actuality, she was most likely performing a ritual cleansing after she had counted seven days from her period. This is why we know the baby would *have to* have been David's, as she hadn't had sex with Uriah after her period... only David. Since she bathed upon her roof, it is possible she had a *mikveh* there, a cleansing pool that fills naturally from rain. According to Tirzah Meacham, "Immersion of the entire body at one time was required. The pool had to be filled with water that was collected naturally, that is, the water could not be drawn and poured into the pool. The pool could be constructed in such a manner as to collect rain, spring water, or water from a river."[1] If this is what Bathsheba was doing, it was neither sensual nor a deliberate act of temptation. In fact, the Hebrew word used to describe her actions on the rooftop is *rachats*, which plainly means "to wash." Most people bathed on their rooftops—a common practice. We know from the text that David was supposed to be campaigning in a war, but he chose not to go. In his idle state (after taking a nap), he scans the horizon and then takes note of her. She would not have been aware of his glance.

It's also important to note that God gave David avenues of escape. He did not have to scan the rooftops, but he did. He did not have to be a peeping tom, but he chose to be. He did not have to inquire about who she was, but he did. He did not have to summon her, but he did. He did not have to force himself upon her, but he did. Every avenue sin provided, he gladly walked into. The great shepherd of Israel, through a series of increasingly damning choices, became a predator.

When the messengers arrived to take Bathsheba, the word "took" (*lāqah*) in the Hebrew means "to take and carry along," "to take possession of," "to take, capture, seize," "carry off," "to be removed," or "to be stolen from."[2] Even more telling, it can also mean to "take in marriage." Bathsheba had no rights, no way to escape this kind of manhandling. She could not protest, though she was already Uriah's wife. She had to comply.

When the passage reminds us that David lay with Bathsheba, it is careful not to say they lay with one another. The Hebrew verbs here are only used in the Bible together in the context of rape. *Lāqah* (which we unpacked above) means to take or steal. *Shakav* means "to lie." While the second verb can connote sexual intercourse, it is primarily used in the rape narratives of the Old Testament.[3] According to Deuteronomy 22:25–27, David deserved to die for his offense: "But if the man meets the engaged woman out in the country, and he rapes her, then only the man must die. Do nothing to the young woman; she has committed no crime worthy of death. She is as innocent as a murder victim. Since the man raped her out in the country, it must be assumed that she screamed, but there was no one to rescue her."

While David's violation of Bathsheba occurred in the palace, the situation was the same. Even if she screamed, who would rescue her? There was no one above David, save God Almighty, who could speak back to the king and rescue her.

Ironically, in the entire narrative, only Uriah refuses to obey the king's edicts. It's important to note that all the members of David's trusted inner circle fought in the conflict, leaving him alone with no accountability. Only servants remained at the palace, and they would have no authority (as Uriah did) to defy the commands of the king. David made a deliberate choice to isolate. He let his lethargy reign. And the results of those two choices had dire consequences.

Grief follows Bathsheba throughout this narrative. While the Bible is silent on whether she and Uriah had children, I believe there's a strong case to make that she had no other children. When Nathan the prophet confronts David, his allegory involves a man and his little lamb, but not a ewe with other little lambs. When David sends for Bathsheba to become another one of his wives, there is no mention of children following her into the palace. Had Bathsheba and Uriah been barren, then Bathsheba's pain would be more complicated. The very thing she longed for (pregnancy) is the very evidence of her violation. Whereas a baby should be the product of love between two married people, this unnamed baby indicates otherwise.

Nine months follow the scene where David "comforts" his wife after the loss of their child. The word *comfort* in the Hebrew is instructive here. *Nacham* means to console, but it also has connotations of grief and repentance for what one has done, particularly to others.[4] Perhaps we see the final stage of David's broken repentance in the aftermath of his child's demise. All that chaos, all the hiding, and his murderous plot reveal that his sin is not simply against God, but against people in his kingdom—Bathsheba and Uriah—and his son bears the consequences. It's instructive to see that they named their second son *Solomon*, which means "man of peace." God's name for the boy, *Jedidiah*, means "beloved of the Lord." This man of peace, beloved of the Lord, would perhaps bring peace and belovedness back into the kingdom after such a breach of reckless sin.

God blessed Bathsheba with more children after Solomon: Shimea, Shobab, and Nathan (obviously not Nathan the prophet).

Scripture indicates that Bathsheba and Solomon had a special bond. In 1 Kings 2:19, we see Bathsheba interceding with Solomon for Adonijah, another of David's sons, who tried to usurp the kingdom. Take note of how he responds to her: "So Bathsheba went to King Solomon to speak on Adonijah's behalf. The king rose from his throne to meet her, and he bowed down before her. When he sat down on his throne again, the king ordered that a throne be brought for his mother, and she sat at his right hand."

Knowing what we do about kings and authority, that Solomon bowed before his mother was a great nod to her prominence in the kingdom. That she sat upon a throne indicates vindication and restoration.

There is speculation that Solomon is the same person as King Lemuel, who wrote Proverbs 31. If that is true, then Bathsheba is the woman he heralds. (We will look at her more in depth in Chapter Eight.)

We see Bathsheba appear in the lineage of Jesus Christ. She is not typically named, though some translations take that liberty. Matthew 1:6 in the NET Bible says, "Jesse the father of David the king. David was the father of Solomon (by the wife of Uriah)." Again, we see no blame leveled at Bathsheba—David is the one who stole Uriah's wife, then murdered his friend. The Apostle Matthew says she was first and foremost the wife of another. He points to David's treachery, not Bathsheba's "seductive" ways. This was not adultery as some have asserted—consensual extramarital sex; it was assault. It has all the hallmarks of rape, which is a heinous abuse of power.

And yet, Bathsheba rose above the trauma. She became a confidant to her son-king. She received a throne. And her blood coursed through the One who would save all from their traumas and trials.

How Does This Apply to Misunderstood You?

There are two ways Bathsheba is misunderstood.

First, she is assigned bad motives by scholars who label her a temptress. She is not alive to correct the record or defend herself. Imagine having your legacy misconstrued for millennia. This is Bathsheba's lot.

As we discussed earlier in this book, it is nearly impossible to control everyone's perceptions of you, particularly when someone has a confirmation bias against you. You could spend your entire life trying not to be misunderstood, but that effort would be better placed in more productive activities. Imagine if you spent your time worrying about and currying favor with enemies who only assumed the worst about you. To do so would border on self-absorption, and it would stymie you from doing the real work God has for you in His Kingdom. If the enemy of your soul can hog-tie your emotions and efforts through frenetic reputation management, you are of little use in building God's great Kingdom. You will have divided loyalties. Life is too short to be consumed by the opinions of others.

Paul reminds us of some sobering truth: "Obviously, I'm not trying to win the approval of people, but of God. If pleasing people were my goal, I would not be Christ's servant" (Galatians 1:10). Being a people-pleaser is antithetical to serving Jesus Christ. The question becomes: are you more concerned about how others view you, or are you consumed with the tasks Christ has set before you? Instead of viewing this negatively, consider this proactive approach: God has created you to do amazing things. According to Ephesians 2:10, you are His masterpiece, endowed with abilities to do good in this world. "For we are God's masterpiece. He has created us anew in Christ Jesus, so we can do the good things he planned for us long ago." Shifting your focus from the negative (what other people think of you) toward the positive (what does God have for me to do?) will revolutionize your joy.

Bathsheba could have allowed rumors and innuendo to keep her from living her life. She could have shrunk into the inner chambers of the palace, living in the shame and pain of what happened to her. But Scripture indicates she moved on. She played a vital role in the nation of Israel. Her son sought her advice as he led the nation. She mothered other children. She outlived her husband.

The other way Bathsheba is misunderstood (and underestimated) comes through King David. He does not see her as one who bears the image of the Most High. He does not consider her value. He sees her merely as property, as a means to quench his sexual appetite in the moment. He chooses not to see her as a person. Note that there was no conversation between them when he assaulted her. She must've known she could not scream, or even if she did, her cries would be left unheeded. Had they communicated, David would've had to acknowledge her humanity. But he did not; instead, she became like livestock to him. Like the little lamb in Nathan's narrative, both she and Uriah were simply pawns in David's commitment to sin and coverup.

Nathan's parable highlighted this.

> There were two men in a certain town. One was rich, and one was poor. The rich man owned a great many sheep and cattle. The poor man owned nothing but one little lamb he had bought. He raised that little lamb, and it grew up with his children. It ate from the man's own plate and drank from his cup. He cuddled it in his arms like a baby daughter. One day a guest arrived at the home of the rich man. But instead of killing an animal from his own flock or herd, he took the poor man's lamb and killed it and prepared it for his guest. (2 Samuel 12:2–4)

Ironic that a story about livestock illuminates David's hypocrisy in his treatment of a human being. He who shepherded sheep, now tasked with shepherding the nation of Israel, has a visceral response to the demise of this fictitious little lamb: "'As surely as the Lord lives,' he vowed, 'any man who would do such a thing deserves to die! He must repay four lambs to the poor man for the one he stole and for having no pity'" (2 Samuel 12:5–6).

David saw the unjust treatment of an animal, yet he could not see his far more egregious sin against an image bearer of God. Later Nathan delivered the truth God had revealed to him: "Why, then, have you despised the word of the Lord and done this horrible deed? For you have murdered Uriah the Hittite with the sword of the Ammonites and stolen his wife" (2 Samuel 12:9).

David dehumanized Bathsheba. And when someone is relegated to being a piece of property, all "livestock" becomes easy to harm. To demean someone like this is to de-soul them, to take away their dignity, their very real humanity.

This kind of misunderstanding is exceptionally difficult to overcome. How does one who has been deemed worthless insist upon her worth? How do we convince a victimizer of our value? In most cases, we cannot. When predatory people dehumanize their victims, they have usually practiced for a long time in their thoughts already. Over years, that erosive thought life becomes a deep canyon, and crawling out of that pit becomes very difficult, almost impossible.

I experienced Bathsheba's brokenness. As a sexual abuse survivor who suffered multiple attacks while living as an only child in an unsafe home full of neglect (which is its own form of dehumanization), I could not force my attackers or neglectors to see my humanity. It began when I was only five years old.

The only pathway I've found back to knowing my worth has been to understand the heart of God toward the broken and powerless. When oppressors oppress, God takes note. When predators prey upon others, God sees. When little girls are raped, God aches alongside them. This does not mean existential questions like "Why did this happen to me?" or "Why didn't God rescue me?" will never arise. Sadly, on this terrible, beautiful earth, sin still reigns. Predatory people exercise their malicious free will. But this period in time is not all there is. We are living on a pinpoint in eternity, a tiny dot. On the other side, God will make all things right. He will wipe away the many tears we cried. And, be assured, He takes note of every inhumanity toward humanity from His throne in Heaven.

Consider these promises about the quartet of the vulnerable (widows, orphans, the poor, and aliens). These people groups are constantly dehumanized, without power and often without hope. Yet God cares for them. When predatory people of the world prey on the vulnerable, they will have to answer to the God of the vulnerable.

> He gives justice to the oppressed
> and food to the hungry.
> The LORD frees the prisoners.
> The LORD opens the eyes of the blind.
> The LORD lifts up those who are weighed down.
> The LORD loves the godly.
> The LORD protects the foreigners among us.
> He cares for the orphans and widows,
>   but he frustrates the plans of the wicked. (Psalm 146:7–9)

> What sorrow awaits the unjust judges
> and those who issue unfair laws.
> They deprive the poor of justice
> and deny the rights of the needy among my people.
> They prey on widows
> and take advantage of orphans.
> What will you do when I punish you,
> when I send disaster upon you from a distant land?
> To whom will you turn for help?

Where will your treasures be safe?
You will stumble along as prisoners
or lie among the dead.
But even then the LORD's anger will not be satisfied.
His fist is still poised to strike. (Isaiah 10:1–4)

But I will be merciful only if you stop your evil thoughts
and deeds and start treating each other with justice; only
if you stop exploiting foreigners, orphans, and widows;
only if you stop your murdering; and only if you stop
harming yourselves by worshiping idols. (Jeremiah 7:5–6)

Do not oppress widows, orphans, foreigners, and the poor.
And do not scheme against each other. (Zechariah 7:10)

Though we see God's heart toward those who are dehumanized
described in the Old Testament, Jesus *demonstrates* it. He goes out of
his way to speak to a woman broken by life (the Samaritan woman at
the well). He offers compassion to the woman caught in adultery. He
aligns himself with the downtrodden and poor, having no place to lay
his head. He finds the marginalized, those who are not considered
worthy of notice, and eats with them, thus validating their worth. In
fact, His harshest words are toward those who look down on others,
whose religious elitism causes them to dismiss the broken.

Post-crucifixion and resurrection, we see the church grappling
with this same predicament:

My dear brothers and sisters [the author of James writes],
how can you claim to have faith in our glorious Lord Jesus
Christ if you favor some people over others? For example,
suppose someone comes into your meeting dressed in fancy
clothes and expensive jewelry, and another comes in who

is poor and dressed in dirty clothes. If you give special attention and a good seat to the rich person, but you say to the poor one, "You can stand over there, or else sit on the floor"—well, doesn't this discrimination show that your judgments are guided by evil motives? Listen to me, dear brothers and sisters. Hasn't God chosen the poor in this world to be rich in faith? Aren't they the ones who will inherit the Kingdom he promised to those who love him? (James 2:1–5)

This is how the Church *should* be. Why? Because that is how God is.

If you have struggled under the tyranny of another's dehumanization, there is hope. Regardless of how you've been treated (and I'm so sorry you've walked that path), the truth is God will perfectly mete out justice on the other side. And on this earth, as you await that moment, you can rest in knowing that despite the fickle and inaccurate opinions of others, you are worthy. You are weighted with glory. You are worth being loved, protected, sought after, and noticed. To truly believe this is to retrain your mind.

Romans 12:2 teaches us how to do this. Paul writes, "Don't copy the behavior and customs of this world, but let God transform you into a new person by changing the way you think. Then you will learn to know God's will for you, which is good and pleasing and perfect." The behavior and customs of this world tend toward dehumanization. They chip away at a person's worth, basing it on fleeting things like looks, personality, and intelligence. The world's system is one of eugenics (the pseudoscience the Nazis used to prove that some people were worth more than others).

But that is not the truth.

The truth? You bear the weight of God's glory, even if you've encountered the worst humanity can throw at you. You are meant for more. A predator's actions or words against you cannot steal what God has indelibly marked on your soul. The devil cannot steal your birthright as a child of God. Circumstances, though egregious, cannot negate the truth that you bear the image of the Almighty God. Learning to fit into that beautiful truth is a lifelong journey. We grow into it, realizing from glory to glory that we carry within us the very Holy Spirit of God. We are His temple, His dwelling place, laced with valor and hope.

You are not the sum of your violations. You are the recipient of a thousand loves, graced to you by a benevolent, seeing God, who will make all things right on the other side of eternity. Rest your heart there. Find solace there.

Truths about Fully Understood You

- Even in trauma, God is working.
- Shame does not belong to victims; it belongs to victimizers.
- Even complicated, pain-laced stories have beauty, including yours.
- After death and grief, God still brings snippets of light and life.
- You are not defined by your tragedy, but by the thoughts of the One who loves you.

Questions for Discussion

1. What gripped you about this retelling of Bathsheba's story? Which details surprised you?
2. How has your opinion about King David changed after today's reading? How has it remained the same?
3. What about Nathan the prophet's story and his interaction with David gives you hope?

4. What choices could David have made instead of preying on another man's wife and having her husband killed? Were there any choices Bathsheba could have made in that situation? Why or why not?

5. Bathsheba had a life after David assaulted her. How does this hint at the Gospel?

CHAPTER SEVEN

Tamar, the Violated One

Virginal Tamar was chaste, kindhearted, and had a bright hope for her future as the daughter of King David. Sister to Absalom, she spent her days near the palace learning the arts and finding joy in both her benevolent duties and her status as a protected princess. One day, Father approached her.

"Amnon is ill," he told her. "He is asking for you. Would you accommodate his needs? He is hungry and needs your kindhearted attention."

"Yes, my father," she said, her voice echoing off the palace walls.

"Oh, and he needs you to feed him," Father said.

This last revelation struck her as odd. Why would Amnon need such direct attention? *He must be very infirm*, she thought, *perhaps at the point of death.*

This worried her as she entered Amnon's house. Her stomach knotted, and her breath came in sips. Something in the room felt far too still, and a sense of dread washed over her. She announced herself as she entered Amnon's bedchamber. Though his own servants stood nearby, his eyes followed her, tracing her body. "Hello, Tamar," he said.

She nodded a greeting in return, but her stomach continued to warn her that something was amiss.

With Amnon clearly still alive, she went to the kitchen, where she steadied herself with tasks. Fetched the freshly milled flour. Added water. Kneaded till elastic. Let it sit. Dredged the lamb shank in aromatics. Sent it out to be grilled. Rolled out flatbread. Asked a servant to place each disc upon the coals as well. Poured olive oil into a shallow bowl, adding garlic and greens. Everything she did, she performed dutifully, as she had done a thousand times. Except this time, she felt her life hanging in the balance.

When Amnon's favorite meal was cooked through, she arranged the lamb, flatbread, and herbed olive oil on a tray and took it to him. "Here's your meal," she said. She placed it on a table near his bed and readied herself to leave. She hoped he had forgotten about the "feeding him" part of his request—or perhaps Father had been wrong? Perhaps he had misheard such a strange request? She pulled her *palla* over her head and turned away.

"No!" Amnon shouted. He pushed away the tray, forcing her to grab it before all the food toppled to the floor. "Everyone get out of here!" he shouted at the servants.

They all left.

Tamar's heart thrummed in panic beneath her ribcage. What could this mean? She tried to leave with the servants, hoping all of this was the whim of a sick half-brother.

"Now bring the food into my bedroom and feed it to me here."

She heard his words and knew she had to obey.

Tamar re-presented the meal to him as he reclined on his bed, placing the tray on his lap. She tore some flatbread, dipped it into the garlic-and-herb olive oil, and fed him a bite. He ate the morsel from her fingers, then grabbed her hand.

Tamar tried to back away, but Amnon grabbed both her wrists. The tray between them crashed to the ground. She hoped the servants weren't too far away to hear the crash. She looked behind her, but no one appeared.

Amnon let out a guttural growl. "Come to bed with me, my darling sister," he snarled.

"No, my brother!" she cried. "Don't be foolish! Don't do this to me!" She had hoped reminding him of his brother status would snap him out of his mania and back to sanity. But his grip tightened, and his breath came in hungry gulps. She tried to free herself from his grip, but she could not. She found her words. "Such wicked things aren't done in Israel," she shouted, hoping someone, *anyone*, would hear her desperation. But no one came to her rescue. "Where could I go in my shame?" she asked, but he now pulled her to himself. Tamar turned her head away from him as he tried to kiss her. "And you would be called one of the greatest fools in Israel," she said, now pleading. She hoped this would level his pride or rouse his logic, but he grabbed at her tunic, ripping it from her shoulder. She gasped.

"Please," she implored, "just speak to the king about it, and he will let you marry me." At least that would get her out of this dangerous, traumatic, shameful situation.

But her words meant nothing. It was as if she spoke to a wall. She was trapped.

Tamar closed her eyes. She tried to imagine her childhood, when she and Amnon had run innocent races around the olive groves. But there was nothing innocent about this competition, and Amnon won. Brutally and quickly.

Afterward, he backed away. His eyes, no longer full of arousal, now held hatred. He spat in Tamar's tear-streaked face, holding her hands so she could not wipe his saliva away. He pushed her. She fell backward onto the cold, hard floor, her clothing in piles around her.

She tried to cover herself, grabbing at her tunic, but her hands suddenly went numb and would not obey her will.

Amnon stood above her, a cruel smirk on his face. "Get. Out. Of. Here." His words hissed snakelike—cruel and calculated.

Tamar found her wits as her hands finally obeyed her. She gathered clothing to herself, covering her nakedness, while she bled onto the floor. "No, no!" Knowing her precarious predicament, she begged, "Sending me away now is worse than what you've already done to me." She would live in disgrace, unmarried and violated, for the rest of her life. Though the thought of marrying such a brute sickened her, it was the only path available to preserve any of her dignity.

Amnon was a bronze statue, unmoved by her plea.

He paced to the entryway of his chamber, hollering for a servant to come.

Tamar pulled on her long, beautiful robe. She shivered, though the day had been unseasonably warm, as the servant appeared.

"Throw this woman out, and lock the door behind her!" Amnon yelled.

The servant obeyed. He grabbed her—no longer "my sister Tamar" but *this woman*—then pushed her out of the house. She fell with a thud to the hard earth. She heard the clank of the outer lock being forced in place. She pounded on the door, crying, but no one came to her rescue. Her sandals were still in Amnon's lair, and she felt the sand beneath her toes as she continued to shake, bleed, and weep, wetting the sand beneath her with tears and blood.

Tamar looked down at the beautiful robe relegated only for the king's daughters—finely woven with purple and scarlet threads, the envy of every young Israelite girl. She remembered wearing it with honor in long promenades in the City of David, and how people would bow as she passed by. All that honor? Destroyed.

She found a break in the robe at her neck. She pulled away a thread, leaving a vulnerable spot in the fabric. She placed that piece in her mouth, clenching it with her teeth, then pulled with the remaining strength she had.

Rip.

The garment divided in half, exposing her underclothes beneath. She threw off the robe now, then sat upon it in the dust. She ripped a strip away, cursing her shame. Then another. She shredded the garment until it was a pile of thready ribbons under the hot Judean sun. No one noticed this. No one stopped to understand or help while she grabbed the pile of fabric and threw it into the outdoor oven. Still crying, Tamar watched her royal covering burn until embers and ashes formed. With no thought for its heat, she bent low to the stove's mouth and ferreted ashes from below. Her hands burned in the effort, but she didn't seem to mind. As the ashes cooled, she gathered them to herself, then heaped them upon her head, wishing they would scald away her beautiful hair. She smeared ashes on her face, even as her tears streamed black.

She finally turned for home, without outer clothing, head and face ashen.

Back at the palace, Absalom approached her. "Is it true that Amnon has been with you?"

Through tears and hysterics, she nodded. *Everyone must know.*

"Well, my sister," Absalom said. "Keep quiet for now, since he's your brother. We don't want to ruin his reputation—he's Father's favorite."

Tamar had no way of resolving her situation, she knew. Her only recourse was to live with her disgrace inside the shelter of Absalom's house. Even Father said nothing about it, cementing her lot. This would be her life. Like her beautiful robe torn to shreds and burnt to ashes, the old carefree princess died, replaced by the violated, unclean "this woman" who would live in hiding the rest of her ashen days.

Two years passed in this way.

Absalom eventually took vengeance upon Amnon, inviting him to a feast with his brothers and lulling him into a drunken stupor before he killed him. But this did nothing to restore Tamar's honor or improve her lot in life.

With Absalom fleeing to his grandfather's house in Geshur, and Father weeping over the loss of Amnon, Tamar felt her future set itself in stone.

The Biblical Narrative

Tamar is the daughter of King David and Maacah, the princess of Geshur (one of his many wives). Tamar is violated and then wears her devastation for a lifetime. Sadly, hers is not a redemptive story. But the fact that it remains in the pages of the Bible is instructive. We have to ask ourselves why it's there and what we are to make of it.

Tamar's name means "date palm," a beautiful, symmetrical Palestinian tree with roots as deep as its branches are wide. It connotes stateliness and desirability.

But in Tamar's tragic story, we see none of this. For Tamar, there is only bereavement and disgrace.

Like the patriarch Joseph, Tamar wears a beautiful robe; it marks her as a princess, as one who is to be favored and honored. This kind of robe extended to the floor, covering both wrists and ankles (making it expensive). It showed that a person did not have to labor—a garment indicating love and privilege. The robe symbolized the tradition of royal daughters being strictly protected. Tamar would have been watched by harem eunuchs, not allowed outside the walls of her compound unless accompanied by others.

Because she is inaccessible to Amnon, he has to resort to trickery to get her alone. He tells his cousin Jonadab, "I am in love with Tamar, my brother Absalom's sister" (2 Samuel 13:4). Note that he removes himself from his relationship with her. He calls her the sister of Absalom, though he too is her brother. He is well aware of the law that forbids such a liaison: "Do not have sexual relations with your stepsister, the daughter of any of your father's wives, for she is your sister" (Leviticus 18:11). This reveals his utter disregard for the Law and his passion to satisfy his lusts. Jonadab then concocts the plan that results in Tamar's rape, telling Amnon, "I'll tell you what to do. Go back to bed and pretend you are ill. When your father comes to see you, ask him to let Tamar come and prepare some food for you. Tell him you'll feel better if she prepares it as you watch and feeds you with her own hands" (2 Samuel 13:5).

Though Tamar is noteworthy as a sister and a princess, we learn through this story that she has honor without power. Her prestige cannot protect her from Jonadab's craftiness or her half-brother's strength and violence. Tamar never knows of this incestuous plot, but the Scriptures reveal it beforehand. She is the blindsided actor in a tragic story.

Sadly, though King David is wise, he unwittingly participates in Amnon's strange charade by commanding Tamar to nurse his son. After all, firstborn sons matter in a king's dynasty. The crown prince's health is tantamount.

And yet, Tamar's kindhearted, obedient nature shines through. She does not protest her father's peculiar suggestion. Instead, she obeys—until all the servants are sent away, leaving her with no protection, and Amnon commences his incestuous assault. That's when she firmly says no, with sincerity and verbal prowess, revealing both her resolve and her intelligence. Prince Amnon does not heed her words; her articulate intelligence only inflames his wickedness. His brute strength overpowers her; she cannot fight back. His "love" morphs into hate the moment he violates her, proving it was merely and only lust. Lust satisfied gives birth to contempt. And suddenly, Tamar's mere presence reminds Amnon of his blatant sin. Besides, she is no longer able to get married; with her virginity gone, she is considered "ruined."

What is worse is that he ruins her life by forcing her to leave. He calls her "this woman." She is not treated with even the respect expected for an Israelite commoner. She is not shown any kind of deference as Amnon's relative, let alone his sister. He does not treat her as a princess. She is nonhuman, an object to be discarded.

Though Tamar tries to plead with Amnon to ask King David to allow a marriage, he refuses, essentially allowing his crime against her to continue in perpetuity. Though Scripture does provide a way forward in the Law ("If a man seduces a virgin who is not engaged to anyone and has sex with her, he must pay the customary bride price and marry her. But if her father refuses to let him marry her, the man must still pay him an amount equal to the bride price of a virgin" [Exodus 22:16–17])—this path is ignored. Note that Amnon violates Tamar; he does not "seduce" her. However, Tamar knows her Law and has the wherewithal to invoke it, hoping her dishonorable half-brother will at least listen to reasoning. He does not.

It is beautiful to note that Tamar never accepts the blame for Amnon's act. It is his violation alone that has ruined her. It is solely his fault, but she has to bear the consequences of his sin by herself. In this way, she becomes an archetype of Christ, who was "despised and rejected—a man of sorrows, acquainted with deepest grief" (Isaiah 53:3a). Though innocent, she suffers. Similarly, "For God made Christ, who never sinned, to be the offering for our sin, so that we could be made right with God through Christ" (2 Corinthians 5:21).

Rending a garment as she does her beautiful robe is a sign of anguish. We see this action in Genesis 37:29, when Reuben peered into the cistern where Joseph was once held captive before being sold to the slave traders. He also tore his clothes in grief. Joseph's father Jacob did the same thing when he learned of Joseph's alleged demise. Job's similar response came after everything had been stripped from him and his children all died. David ripped his garments when he learned of Saul and Jonathan's deaths. Elisha mourned this way when Elijah was taken up into Heaven. Mordecai ripped his garments when he learned of Haman's plot to destroy the Jews. Tearing one's clothes meant the deepest kind of grief. Today Jewish people continue the practice, calling it *keriah*. "Today's ritual is less spontaneous and more regulated: the garment is cut by a rabbi at a funeral service, as the bereaved recite words relating to God's sovereignty. One tradition says that the mourner must tear the clothing over the heart—a sign of a broken heart."[1] Certainly, Tamar's heart was ripped in two.

Tamar's brother, Prince Absalom, attempts to silence her. He reasons, "Well, my sister, keep quiet for now, since he's your brother" (2 Samuel 13:20). I've taken the artistic license to fill in the rest of his quote to make it clear that he doesn't mean, "Don't worry about it, I'll take care of this for you and do what I can to restore your honor." Though he does kill Amnon in revenge two years later, it is an act born of bitterness, which serves only to further fracture both his family and David's budding dynasty. How many rape victims have heard these same admonitions? Sadly, this silencing is commonplace. People prefer to sweep rape under the rug, particularly when it occurs within a family structure. Best to keep the secret in order to maintain the family's standing. I would argue that silence and secrecy are like cancers that eat away at a family's strength, and we see only devastation after David's assault on Bathsheba and Amnon's subsequent rape of Tamar. In the Bible, when rape occurs, violence, strife, and war follow.

The pattern in David's family is instructive: David violates Bathsheba. He woos Uriah back to the castle, getting him drunk. Eventually, he forces the faithful Uriah to the front lines, resulting in his death. His son Amnon violates Tamar. Absalom waits until Amnon is drunk, then murders him. Surely the sins of the father are visited upon his sons.

King David, who was known to rout the Philistines and who had attacked Israel's enemies with vengeful force, had a pallid response to Tamar's rape. The Scripture only says this: "When King David heard what had happened, he was very angry" (2 Samuel 13:21). In the Dead Sea Scrolls and the Greek version, there's a curious addition. "But he did not punish his son Amnon, because he loved him, for he was his firstborn." In short, he preferred his firstborn son to the cries of his young daughter. His anger did not enact punishment or any sort of restorative justice. His inaction proved he valued the status quo over doing the right thing, preferring the perpetrator over the victim. (This is an ancient pattern that exists in full force today.) Perhaps, too, we have to take into account his own nefarious actions toward Bathsheba: if he condemned Amnon, he would have to recondemn himself. Though King David was "very angry," the Scripture says he does not weep over the travesty. Instead, he "mourned many days for his son Amnon" (2 Samuel 13:37).

Note that every element of perpetration involves the men in this narrative. Tamar, the violated one, is the only one who deals valiantly with her attacker. She resists. She says no. She tries in vain to reason with him. Even the servants (who, since they served Amnon, were most likely male) did not rescue Tamar, but forcefully sent her away.

There is a small thread of redemption in this story. Absalom, though he is not required to do so, takes Tamar in. He keeps her protected and cared for in his household. One can imagine she has a positive impact on her extended family, because we read in 2 Samuel 14:27 something curious. Absalom "had three sons and one daughter. His daughter's name was Tamar, and she was very beautiful." She is named after her aunt Tamar, whose brothers remain unnamed.

How Does This Apply to Misunderstood You?

Tamar understood her situation as it unfolded. She knew that Amnon's violation would hurt her forever. She understood her community, the kingdom, and how a violated virgin princess would fare within that context. Just as King David grossly misunderstood Bathsheba, ignoring her humanity, so Amnon did here. Tamar was obviously misunderstood by both Amnon and Jonadab. She was treated only as an object of lust. She was looked upon inhumanely, with cool disdain and pure evil.

But I want to focus on something else—a little sentence you may have missed in the narrative. "So Tamar lived as a desolate woman in her brother Absalom's house" (2 Samuel 13:20). I would contend that Tamar misunderstood herself. She misunderstood her value in an economy that cemented her lack of worth. In other words, she believed the lie that she could not be redeemed from this situation.

While she had little recourse and certainly no authority to right the wrongs committed against her, she did not need to live under the adjective *desolate*. Even though men had actively forsaken her, the God who formed her in her mother Maacah's womb had not and would not. Perhaps Absalom knew this as well, which could be why he named his daughter after her—as a proclamation of hope, a statement that things do not always have to be as they seem.

What do we do when the person who misunderstands us *is* us? What if we have positioned ourselves to believe lies because society cements them as truth? Tamar's community deemed her desolate, and she walked that path. And yet, as we look at the redemptive ability of God, we know that He had more for Tamar than desolation. His was the consolation of knowing. He saw her predicament. He knew her anguish. His heart beat for people like her; she resembled the quartet of the vulnerable as, in a sense, she was a widow, bereft of a husband. She no longer lived under the protection of her father, who essentially orphaned her when he chose his predatory son over her honor. No longer a princess of the king, Tamar was robbed of the slim measure of privilege she had once possessed. Though she now lived under Absalom's protection, his resources were his, not hers. In this way, she was poor—like nearly all other women of her time.

From previous chapters, we know God is touched by those who are exploited, and the penalty for exploiting others was severe in those days. We see God's judgment on the house of David for his sin against

Bathsheba and Amnon's sin against Tamar. They did not escape consequence.

Though no doubt difficult to discern, God's ultimate favor rested upon His daughter Tamar. Like her, we too are fighting to understand our true identity as princesses of the King, as the world tries everything in its power to destroy our souls. Remember, the system of this world, though passing away, is under the jurisdiction of the evil one, Satan, whose chief job is to lie to us. If he can get us to believe we are desolate and to misunderstand our standing before God, he will render us useless for the kingdom of our true King.

Perhaps the most insidious misunderstanding comes when we, like Tamar, sink into our perceived worthlessness—when we believe a lie. To misunderstand our place in God's family, forgetting His affection for us, is to pull the plug on hope.

The truth? Yes, we have endured much. Yes, people have hurt us. Yes, life has not tilted the way we wanted it to. Yes, we suffer under the weight of other people's cruelties, sins, and misdeeds. Yes, we can be nearly broken by life. But there's a better yes. Paul illuminates this in 2 Corinthians 1:20–22. Let his words remind you of the *yeses* God has for you:

> For all of God's promises have been fulfilled in Christ with a resounding "Yes!" And through Christ, our "Amen" (which means "Yes") ascends to God for his glory. It is God who enables us, along with you, to stand firm for Christ. He has commissioned us, and he has identified us as his own by placing the Holy Spirit in our hearts as the first installment that guarantees everything he has promised us.

Friend, there is hope. We simply need to remind ourselves of the truth brought to us through Jesus Christ. He has fulfilled every promise offered to humankind, including a reversal of soul fortune. No longer living under the terrible word *desolate*, we can say yes to God's power. We can say yes to standing firm in the footprints of Christ. We can say yes to His commissioning (we are not disqualified!). We can say yes to the constant companion of the Holy Spirit living within us. We can say yes to the promises of God on our behalf.

Jesus secured a new identity for us. No longer forsaken, but sought. No longer living on the margins of life, but brought into the action of the Kingdom. No longer saddled with guilt and shame from the past, but redeemed and set free.

As we look at Tamar's desolation, it's important we understand the word's meaning. To be desolate is to be destitute or deprived. It's like looking at an empty, lifeless desert. Desolate connotes uninhabited locales, places that have not seen people. It's a wilderness laid waste. According to the *King James Version Dictionary*, it's a place in ruinous condition, completely neglected, forlorn, and destroyed. It can mean "solitary" or "afflicted." In some places, it can even mean being "deserted of God; deprived of comfort." It is a wasted place, a broken branch severed from the tree. It is a land ravaged and left barren. Gloom, sadness, and destitution reign in that place.[2] Daniel prophesies Jerusalem's desolation in Daniel 9. Jesus refers to the Temple's demise this way when He predicts its destruction in Matthew 24. The word means utter and complete ruin.

And yet, we have hope. The truth may be that we have experienced desolation, but there is a truth deeper still—that God loves to rescue the broken, the downtrodden, those laid low. We see hints of this in Isaiah 58 when God reminds a captive Israel that life will not always be full of deprivation:

> The Lord will guide you continually, giving you water when you are dry and restoring your strength. You will be like a well-watered garden, like an ever-flowing spring. Some of you will rebuild the deserted ruins of your cities. Then you

will be known as a rebuilder of walls and a restorer of homes. (Isaiah 58:11–12)

When we misunderstand desolation, making it our permanent state, we don't leave room for God's great intervention. The Gospel, as we look to the New Testament, is about reversal and renewal. The curse against us (sin) is reversed, and our broken, tired souls are renewed by the Holy Spirit within. The old is gone; the new has come (see 2 Corinthians 5:17). While our past may tempt us to despair, it cannot compare to the resurrection power Jesus has secured for our sake. Paul reminds us, "Forgetting the past and looking forward to what lies ahead, I press on to reach the end of the race and receive the heavenly prize for which God, through Christ Jesus, is calling us" (Philippians 3:13–14). The past is gone. Oswald Chambers, in *My Utmost for His Highest*, writes, "Let the past sleep, but let it sleep on the bosom of Christ, and go out into the irresistible future with him."[3] Friend, you may have walked through the slough of despondency, but an irresistible future beckons. Desolation is your past. Consolation is your present. Complete and utter restoration is your future.

Many of us say we understand our redemption from a desolate past, but so few of us really grasp our position in Christ and our inheritance as saints today. Misunderstand this, and we will live a less-than life. We must retrain our minds to believe the truth of what it means to be a Christ-follower. Consider these truths. Meditate upon them. Renew your mind with them. As a follower of Jesus, this is true of you:

- I am a saint. (Ephesians 2:19, Romans 8:27)
- I am adopted as a child of God. (Romans 8:15–17, Ephesians 1:4–5)
- I am saved from my sins. (John 5:24, Romans 10:9–10)
- I am heard. (Jeremiah 29:12–13, 1 Peter 3:12)
- I am loved. (1 John 4:7–11)

- I am redeemed. (Ephesians 1:7)
- I am victorious. (1 John 5:4, 1 Corinthians 15:55–57)
- I am given spiritual gifts. (Ephesians 2:10, 1 Peter 4:10–11)
- I am made new. (Ephesians 4:22–24)
- I am forgiven. (Romans 8:15–17)
- I am reconciled. (Romans 5:10–11)
- I am rewarded. (Galatians 6:9)
- I am a conqueror. (Romans 8:37)
- I am made righteous. (2 Corinthians 5:21)
- I am blessed. (Ephesians 1:3)
- I am made capable. (Philippians 4:13)
- I am light. (Matthew 5:14)
- I am called. (1 Corinthians 7:17)
- I am complete. (Colossians 2:10)
- I am accepted. (Romans 15:7)
- I am created. (Genesis 1:27)
- I am part of Christ's body. (1 Corinthians 12:27)
- I am chosen. (1 Peter 2:9, John 15:16)
- I am the temple of the Holy Spirit. (1 Corinthians 6:19–20)
- I am raised with Christ. (Colossians 3:1–3)
- I am Jesus's friend. (John 15:15)
- I am God's handiwork. (Ephesians 2:10)
- I am a citizen of Heaven. (Philippians 3:20)
- I am a new creation. (2 Corinthians 5:17)
- I am clean. (John 15:3)
- I am free from condemnation. (Romans 8:1)
- I am a joint heir with Christ. (Romans 8:17)
- I am walking a triumphant procession. (2 Corinthians 2:14)
- I am a fragrance. (2 Corinthians 2:15)
- I am being changed into Christ's likeness. (2 Corinthians 3:18)

- I am a minister of reconciliation. (2 Corinthians 5:18–19)
- I am given strength where I am weak. (2 Corinthians 12:9–10)
- I am an heir to God and His Kingdom. (Galatians 3:29)
- I am blessed with every spiritual blessing in Christ. (Ephesians 1:3)
- I am sealed with the Holy Spirit. (Ephesians 1:13)
- I have been rescued from darkness. (Colossians 1:13)
- I am freed from accusation. (Colossians 1:22)
- I am firmly rooted in Christ. (Colossians 2:7)
- I am a child of light. (1 Thessalonians 5:5)
- I am born again. (1 Peter 1:23)
- I am an enemy of Satan. (1 Peter 2:11)
- I am anointed. (1 John 2:27)
- I am purchased. (1 Corinthians 6:20)
- I am granted access to Christ through the Holy Spirit. (Ephesians 2:18)
- I am hidden with Christ in God. (Colossians 3:3)
- I am the recipient of a sound mind. (2 Timothy 1:7)
- I am being perfected. (Philippians 1:6)
- I am full of life. (1 John 5:12)
- I am no longer a slave. (Galatians 4:7)
- I am set free. (John 8:36)
- I am being healed. (1 Peter 2:24)
- I am walking in authority. (Luke 10:19)
- I am established in my faith. (Colossians 2:7)
- I am able to fight spiritual battles. (Mark 16:17–18)
- I am humble and kind. (Colossians 3:12)
- I am an ambassador of Christ. (2 Corinthians 5:20)
- I am complete in Jesus. (Colossians 2:10)
- I am never forsaken or abandoned. (Hebrews 13:5)
- I am bold. (2 Corinthians 3:12)[4]

What powerful truths! What an amazing God we serve. Though our lot in life might be painful and broken, God's great redemption shines before us all. By God's grace, we can move beyond the desolation of the past and lay hold of that which Christ has won for us.

Friend, don't misunderstand your identity. While you cannot control what has been done to you, and you may still struggle under the tyranny of another's choices, you still have free will and a choice before you. This is an ancient choice, placed before those who wandered in the wilderness: a choice between living in the slavery of the past or the freedom of the future. Moses reminded the nation of Israel,

> Today I have given you the choice between life and death, between blessings and curses. Now I call on heaven and earth to witness the choice you make. Oh, that you would choose life, so that you and your descendants might live! You can make this choice by loving the LORD your God, obeying him, and committing yourself firmly to him. This is the key to your life. (Deuteronomy 30:19–20a)

We serve a gentlemanly God, who beckons us toward Him but never forces our hand or will. His invitation is full of life. Don't let past trauma cloud the impetus to move forward. Don't let the many difficulties you've faced make you misunderstand your choices. Your lot is not set in stone—it is fluid, carried along by the River of Life.

I want to return to Tamar's name—a date palm, a tree whose roots grow deep and wide. When I had the opportunity to visit Israel, I learned that date palms start off growing on the ground, meaning they look like a shrub for a few years. Then suddenly they shoot heavenward, and as they grow toward the sun, they produce an amazing, sweet fruit. They are grown from shoots that spring from each mature tree's trunk. Those saplings have to be pried from the mother tree and replanted.

Tamar emulated her name. As a sapling connected to her family of origin, she stayed in its protective environment until Amnon hacked at her soul and severed her from her parents' household. Though Tamar, no doubt, felt anchored to the earth when she lived in Absalom's home, perhaps she grew heavenward as well. And, since Absalom named his daughter after her, perhaps she flourished in this new protective environment. Of course, this is merely speculation.

My prayer for you as you work through your own misunderstanding of who you are is that you'll be like a date palm: supplanted, then replanted in order to grow and bear fruit. This prayer has roots in Scripture. Tamar lived in the era of the Psalms, most of which were composed by her father, David. Imagine her hearing these words:

> Oh, the joys of those who do not follow the advice of the wicked, or stand around with sinners, or join in with mockers. But they delight in the law of the LORD, meditating on it day and night. They are like trees planted along the riverbank, bearing fruit in each season. Their leaves never wither, and they prosper in all they do. (Psalm 1:1–3)

Tamar certainly obeyed these words. She pleaded her case against one who was hell-bent against the Law she loved. Tamar, the date palm, had the potential to sink her roots down deep and flourish. In Ephesians 3:17b–19, we see the root metaphor in play:

> Your roots will grow down into God's love and keep you strong. And may you have the power to understand, as all God's people should, how wide, how long, how high, and how deep his love is. May you experience the love of Christ, though it is too great to understand fully. Then you will be made complete with all the fullness of life and power that comes from God.

Let's endeavor to live up to Tamar's beautiful name, sending roots deep into the soil of God's great affection and love.

In that circle of two between us and the Almighty, we are never misunderstood. Instead, we are set free from disgrace.

Truths about Fully Understood You

- Despite the past, your life can still flourish.
- You are not the sum of the sins committed against you.
- God's grace reaches into your tragedy.
- Trauma need not define you.
- God loves to heal you.

Questions for Discussion

1. Does David's handling of the assault surprise you? What could he have done differently? Why do you think he acted in the way he did?
2. How did Tamar reveal her character in the narrative? What did she do that was honorable?
3. Why did Tamar feel she could never get rid of her disgrace? What aspects of that culture that prevented her from having a fulfilling married life?
4. How does Absalom's response mirror the response of many toward sexual abuse victims today? How does keeping things a secret harm a person? How does it shield them from further injury?
5. Why do you think this story is written in God's word? What can we learn from it?

CHAPTER EIGHT

The Proverbs 31 Woman, the Perfect One

S he picked up her quill, then dipped it in the inkwell on the desk. She pressed nib to papyrus and wrote to her son:

> *O my son, O son of my womb, O son of my vows, do not waste your strength on women, or those who ruin kings. It is not for kings, O Lemuel, to guzzle wine. Rulers should not crave alcohol. For if they drink, they may forget the law and not give justice to the oppressed. Let them drink to forget their poverty and remember their troubles no more.*

She thought of all the subjects populating the kingdom, some of no significance, some of high stature. Her mind lighted on the widows of the land, how helpless and hapless they had become in her world. She dipped her quill back into the ink. "Speak up for those who cannot speak for themselves; ensure justice for those being crushed. Yes, speak up for the poor and helpless, and see they get justice."

These were the words of wisdom she wanted to bless her son with.

She set down the quill as he entered the room. *Such a strong man Lemuel has become!* She rolled the papyrus, tying it with a linen cord she had woven. "For the future," she said. "When you are in want of a wife."

"Thank you, Mother," Lemuel said. He sat before her, and then smiled. "You are always taking my wellbeing to heart."

"Aye, that is my purpose now." She almost added, "Now that your father has passed," but the grief still felt thickened, and she worried she would weep. So instead, she took a deep breath. In the quiet companionship between mother and son, she contemplated her own life, how she had scrabbled her way into society and the city gates. Though she knew her own example spanned a lifetime, she tried to encapsulate everything a wife could be in her words to her son.

She started by asking Lemuel a question. "Who can find a virtuous and capable wife?"

"I hope I may find her," he said.

"That is my prayer as well." She stood and poured two cups of mint tea.

She sat again, facing him. Her world was no different than any era of humanity that had preceded it. How a woman looked, how her hair cascaded, whether her teeth were white and straight, the way she moved in the world—these things caught the attention of men, but appearance was a fickle stabilizer. What really mattered, what stood the test of time and persevered in the years of a marriage, was virtue and industry.

"She needs to have virtue," she said. "A pretty face does not help in times of trouble."

"You have instilled that within me my entire life. But is it wrong to want a woman of beauty?"

She took a long drink of cooling tea. "No, of course not. But just be aware that beauty is simply the skin; it's what's beneath that causes a life."

She fingered the ruby necklace at her throat. "You remember this story, don't you?"

"Yes, when Father spoiled you."

She recalled the affection of her husband. "You are more precious than rubies," he had told her, producing a ruby necklace as an extravagant gift—so extravagant that it made her gasp. She wished he had more sense than that, spending their income on what would not last, but now as she clung to the necklace, she smiled. He had died years ago, but his gift remained a testimony to their enduring connection.

"Your father was a generous man."

The thing she had most wanted after they first shared the marriage bed was to be seen as trustworthy. She wanted her yes to mean yes and her no to mean no. It meant nothing for her to say, "I want you to trust me," if her words did not back up some sentiment.

"A trustworthy woman is necessary," she told her son.

"That is my desire as well."

"I wanted to be that for your father. But first, I knew I had to give myself to the Almighty, asking for wisdom and strength. I remember praying, 'Oh dear Lord, please enrich me so I can enrich my husband. Shape me into the kind of woman who brings him good, not harm, all the days of his life.'"

"Tell me about the lean years again." Lemuel drank his tea while the sun angled through the window way.

"In those early years, I procured wool from our flock of sheep, stripped it of dirt and debris, and collected it for later use. I took note of the areas around our home where wild linseed plants grew, then gathered the stalks to make fabric. Knowing the winter would arrive before most anticipated it, I kept myself busy spinning, spinning, spinning, readying the raw materials into something beautiful to clothe us. I crafted blankets and coverings for our home as a hedge against freezing temperatures. How good God was to supply what I needed to protect our growing family!"

Lemuel nodded, seemingly in thought.

"But life was not merely about eking out a living. I longed for more," she said.

"What do you mean?"

"Throughout my marriage, I pined for variety—it captured me, particularly in the food we all ate. I bartered for spices from afar that I found at the docks near the Great Sea in order to receive precious vials of each substance. I stretched our stores of cinnamon and cloves, scenting our home and the food I placed before you and your father. Lamb tasted better with mint and cumin, I knew. And boiled eggs taste much better with dill."

Lemuel's face lit up, as he remembered the taste of each dish. "I am the grateful recipient of your love for spices," he said.

As dusk pressed in, she reminded her son of the difficult mornings. A wife who rose early would be a blessing, as she had trained herself to do. The world got away from her when she slept beyond dawn, and she regretted what she called her laziness—though her dear husband often praised her when she did manage to awake early. In the wee hours before the sun pinked the sky, she would sing praises to the Almighty as she prepared breakfast for her household. Once finished, she would gather the servant girls and give them tasks for the day. Together, they worked to make their home a haven for many.

Lemuel cleared his throat. "I want my home to be a haven, too."

"That makes me proud, son. I have no doubt it will be."

She then told Lemuel of her pursuits outside the home. Lemuel's father, after observing her discipline and trustworthiness, eventually added to her responsibilities. Knowing that she had a stronger head for business and commerce than he did, he put her in charge of property and farmland. She smiled as she told Lemuel about the first plot of land she had purchased, thanks to money made from the extra clothing she created from wool and flax. The field had a southern exposure and, though rocky, was the perfect spot to plant a vineyard. She touched the small of her back, then, remembering the backbreaking labor, how she lifted rocks by hand, creating a wall around the vineyard. She grafted vines from the best stock in Judea and coddled them as if they were her children. Years later, grape juice and wine rewarded her work.

"In enterprise," she told Lemuel, "the folks in our village knew me as kindhearted, yet shrewd. I had a head for numbers and fairness, and I knew the sacred art of turning a profit, even when I sold the smallest bunch of mint in the marketplace or a cache of honey from a forgotten hive."

As the sun melted into the horizon, she remembered lighting the lamp, grasping the spindle, and spinning thread, her fingers twisting fiber in order to coax a new piece of material to warm her household or sell in town. "In the evenings," she said, "I would talk to Father. We would recount the day together, sharing the best of the day and the worst, laughing often. Though labor-filled, our evenings were the most convivial parts of my day."

"You miss Father, do you not?"

To that, she had no words. How do you explain to a son the ways of companionship they shared?

She changed the direction of their conversation. She rose and refilled their cups before lighting the lamp between them. "I want you to know this first of all: Our God always brought opportunities to serve the broken. My heart ached for those who had little or nothing. It bent toward the widow and the orphan, the alien and the poor. As you know, I continue this beautiful privilege, and I pray often that you will continue in my footsteps."

"Of course, Mother," Lemuel said.

"I want you to know why I do this," she said. "Every single time I offer food or clothing to a person in need, I see the face of God on each person. If you are careful to look beyond the streak of dirt branding a face, or into the vacant eyes of the hungry, the Almighty lives there. To serve them is to serve Him."

As she continued to encourage her son to find a noble wife, she said, "Your father— he was always well-known at the city gates. He had civic responsibilities, and he tended to them well."

"Was he a good man?" her son asked.

She nodded. "Yes, the very best."

"But you, Mother, weren't you known there as well?" Lemuel had a glint in his eye, a teasing quality to his voice.

"I did my part," she said. "Back in the day I created a lot of merchandise—bedspreads, purple gowns fit for royalty, linen garments taken in at the waist, and sashes. The merchants of our village and the surrounding villages knew me and, I am grateful to say, trusted my handiwork."

Lemuel sat back and put his hands behind his head. A smile played on his lips. "I remember Father's song about you."

She blushed, remembering the melody and words.

Lemuel cleared his throat, then sang his baritone best. "She is clothed with strength and dignity, and she laughs without fear of the future. When she speaks, her words are wise, and she gives instructions with kindness." He took a breath, then continued. "She carefully watches everything in her household and suffers nothing from laziness. Her children stand and bless her." At this he stood to his feet, pulled her to standing, and twirled her in the dimming light. "There are many virtuous and capable women in the world, but you surpass them all."

With a flourish and a low trill to his voice, he finished the song. They sat facing each other again. A tear leaked down her cheek. He reached over and wiped it. "Don't cry, Mother. It was a happy song, was it not?"

"The happiest. It made me remember the joy of Father, that is all."

"I miss him too. I hope I can become a husband like him."

"You will, by Almighty's strength." The flicker of lamplight between them reminded her it was time to get back to the spindle, to weave afresh. "One last thing you need to know about your future wife," she told Lemuel.

"What is that?"

"Charm is deceptive, and beauty does not last; but a woman who fears the LORD will be greatly praised." She finished her tea. "Once you find her, do not let her go. And remember to reward her for all she has done, just as your father did. He often praised me, and he did not discourage me from pursuing excellence. He let my deeds publicly declare my praise—something I continue to reap a harvest from even now."

"That is my prayer, my hope." He stood. "Best be finishing the evening work."

She smiled. He had inherited her industriousness. She handed him the linen-tied scroll. "Take this. Read it later," she said.

"Thank you, Mother." He kissed her forehead, then left her abode as crickets sang night songs and she grasped the spindle.

The Biblical Narrative

King Lemuel is unmentioned in the Bible, other than in this passage. He is most likely a pagan king who chose to follow the God of the Israelites.[1] His name means "belonging to God." Some scholars believe this was a pen name, and that Lemuel was Solomon and the Proverbs 31 woman was his mother, Bathsheba. Still, some contend that the Proverbs 31 woman is a metaphor for wisdom. Throughout the book, wisdom is personified, and in this passage, she is fleshed out.

I chose to keep the ambiguity in the story I wrote, playing it out as a scene between a mother and a son because it did feel like the kind of advice a mother would offer a son who is planning to be married someday.

When we work our way past her advice about sexual purity and not overdrinking, we enter the "famous" portion of this passage, verses 10–31. These twenty-two verses are poetic. Like Psalm 119, each verse begins with the next letter of the Hebrew alphabet. It's an acrostic—the ABCs of what a godly woman would look like or how wisdom plays out in a life. This made the passage easy to memorize or recite. According to many scholars, the person who is meant to hear this message and memorize it is a man, not a woman.[2] Take a look at the beginning of Chapter Thirty-One: "The sayings of King Lemuel contain this message, which his mother taught him" (31:1). The first commands in the passage are directed to men (2–9), interrupted by a discourse on the traits of a godly wife, but end again with a directive to men: "Reward her for all she has done. Let her deeds publicly declare her praise" (31).[3]

Women are not the intended audience for this chapter!

There is so much more to the phraseology "virtuous wife." The term is *eseth hayil* in Hebrew, which can also mean "valiant wife," but it is the same phraseology used to describe men of valor in passages like 2 Kings 24:14 and Exodus 18:21. The language connotes a heroic champion, one who enacts victory. This woman is strong, clothed with fortitude.

Consider that this idealized woman of valor truly may be the personification of wisdom when you read, "She is more precious than rubies" (10). The author writes, "Wisdom is more precious than rubies; nothing you desire can compare with her" (Proverbs 3:15).

The issue of trustworthiness enters the vernacular as the mother admonishes the son. A husband has confidence in the virtue of a good wife. Martin Luther is known to have written this about his wife: "The greatest gift of God is a pious amiable spouse who fears God and loves his house, and with whom one can live in perfect confidence."[4] Not only that, but a good wife enriches her spouse—the Hebrew word for this connotes plunder. She brings him wealth. Her goodness is wholehearted, and it lasts throughout her lifetime. In other words, she is unchangeable in her virtue. She is consistent and reliable.

Not only does she possess these inward traits, but outwardly she is industrious and goal-oriented. It's important to note, particularly for our sakes as we compare ourselves to the Proverbs 31 woman, that she does not accomplish all these tasks in one day. The acrostic poem is written in past tense, which means her work is recounted in retrospect, much like an obituary that captures a lifetime rather than a day-in-the-life snapshot. Also note that this woman had servants who helped her accomplish many of these tasks. Hers was not a solitary effort, but a communal one. Note, too, that she treats her servants with the kindness God has required all of Israel to use with outsiders and workers.

When the passage says, "She is clothed with strength and dignity," it's important we look at other translations. Clothing is actually the act of girding, which means to place a belt around your middle in order to strengthen yourself for battle. "It means to get ready for some 'kind of heroic or difficult action,' such as hard running...escape from Egypt...or physical labor."[5] When she spins fibers into thread, she demonstrates her knowledge of the technology available at that time, just like other matriarchs who worked the distaff and spindle—like Sarah, Rebekah, and Rachel.

Unlike the faithless nation of Israel who dismissed the needs of the poor (and were thus forced into exile), this virtuous woman personified the *hesed* of God, the loyal love meant for all human beings. She heeded the words of Isaiah, who wrote, "Learn to do good. Seek justice. Help the oppressed. Defend the cause of orphans. Fight for the rights of widows" (Isaiah 1:17).

This woman is known for her proactive understanding of the coldness of winter and preparing for it. She is like the ant in Proverbs 6:6–8. "Take a lesson from the ants, you lazybones. Learn from their ways and become wise! Though they have no prince or governor or ruler to make them work, they labor hard all summer, gathering food in winter." This woman of valor is self-ruled, and she has the uncanny ability to see the future and prepare for whatever heartache it may bring. The term "scarlet" most likely means "double-layered fabric," able to keep one warm in harsh temperatures.[6] That she creates purple fabrics reveals her ingenuity and her love of fine things. To dye a garment purple, she would have had to procure the dye made from a seashell from the Phoenician coast.[7] She is both wise and extravagant—traits of God Himself.

Her inner life informs her outer work—and that work is done with excellence. It not only helps provide for her household, but it brings positive attention to her husband. She personifies Proverbs 3:3: "Never let loyalty and kindness leave you! Tie them around your neck as a reminder. Write them deep within your heart." When she teaches, the term is *torat hesed*, which means her teaching is always with deep, loyal love as the motive. She is not an angry instructor in a classroom, but a kindhearted messenger to those who want to learn.

We see the importance of fearing God at the end of this passage: "A woman who fears the LORD will be greatly praised" (31:30). While it is not wrong to be beautiful and charming, the mother of Lemuel reminds her son that those traits can fade with age. But a good character lasts forever and has greater significance over a lifetime. This echoes the beginning of the book: Proverbs 1:7 tells us, "Fear of the LORD is the foundation of true knowledge, but fools despise wisdom and discipline." The Proverbs 31 woman underscores the strong connection between fearing God and finding wisdom.

How Does This Apply to Misunderstood You?

While the Proverbs 31 woman was *not* misunderstood by her son Lemuel, she is often misunderstood today. People hold up this ancient woman as a nearly impossible ideal for modern women to follow. We are guilty of superimposing our culture and Western ideas upon her, making her into a perfect saint who works herself to the bone. In short, *we* misunderstand her—to our peril and stress.

Grace and truth are our tools to work through the Proverbs 31 woman's example. Instead of comparing our one bad day to one woman's grand obituary, it's important we offer ourselves the grace God so freely gives us. No doubt the woman recounted in the last chapter of Proverbs had bad days, failed often, and experienced heart-ache and depression. Don't compare your worst struggle with her greatest snapshot of victory. This can apply to all of us, particularly in a social media environment, where Proverbs 31 is personified daily with carefully curated images of perfection and accomplishment.

The truth is, we are all a mess. Sure, we are endowed with hope and the power of the Holy Spirit, but the fact remains that we are clay-footed folks eking out a living and a life as best we know how. We are all on a sanctification journey (as was the Proverbs 31 woman). And one day, the good Lord will completely restore us, giving us new bodies, wiping away every heartache, and rewarding the work we did on this earth for Him. But as we wait in the place between the now and the not yet, we will be far more joyful if we look at our own journey instead of comparing ourselves to someone else's. Consider the wisdom of Paul as he writes to the Galatian church: "Pay careful attention to your own work, for then you will get the satisfaction of a job well done, and you won't need to compare yourself to anyone else. For we are each responsible for our own conduct" (Galatians 6:4–5).

We must rest in the powerful truth that Proverbs 31's audience was not female, but male. It's a poetic, hope-filled list of potential traits a man may seek in a wife, not a laundry list of our personal shortcomings. That it took this woman a lifetime to achieve what she did should also give us pause when we feel we fall short. Anyone would.

She is not perfect, nor are we. And when we are tempted to denigrate ourselves when we fall into weakness, there is a better reversal we can cling to. It's in our inadequacies that Christ has the opportunity to strengthen us. Our weakness in fulfilling our calling as followers of Jesus is the blank canvas on which He paints His most startling work. When we strive after perceived perfection in our own strength, it's like we are fingerpainting madly on a white stretch of cloth. There is no room for the stroke of the Master artist. Our broken state before a perfect God is where we find true perfection—the completeness we find in Jesus Christ.

Paul speaks much of weakness when he encourages believers. His most famous passage is one I've cited often in talks and in books. Paul is complaining about a thorn in the flesh sent to torment him. He begs God three times to remove it from him, but God reminds him of something surprising. Paul's area of torment is where God can do His best work. "Each time he [God] said, 'My grace is all you need. My power works best in weakness'" (2 Corinthians 12:9a). You would think Paul's response would be, "Yes, I get that, but please take this away." No, as Paul grapples with this weakness and pain, he says something surprising. "So now I am glad to boast about my weaknesses, so that the power of Christ can work through me. That's why I take pleasure in my weaknesses, and in the insults, hardships, persecutions, and troubles that I suffer for Christ. For when I am weak, then I am strong" (2 Corinthians 12:9b–10). The words that stand out to me are *so that*. When we know our inadequacy apart from Christ, we fully understand our need for His Spirit within us.

Instead of berating ourselves for failing to live up to an ideal like the Proverbs 31 woman, we can honestly assess our lives and tell the truth about our weakness, *so that* we can tap into the strength we need that is offered readily to the followers of Christ.

Reconsider the traits of the Proverbs 31 woman:

- Virtuous
- Capable
- Trustworthy
- Enriching of others
- Good
- Industrious
- Sacrificial
- Intelligent

- Wise
- Strong
- Kindhearted
- Compassionate
- Faithful
- Faith-filled
- Merciful
- Creative
- Other-focused
- Shepherdlike
- Servant-hearted
- God-fearing

Who does this remind you of?

Jesus embodied all these traits. He lived them. The Proverbs 31 woman is a foreshadowing of Who would come, an other-focused Good Shepherd whose sacrificial life wooed the world to the Father who created us all. His yes was yes. He could be trusted to keep His word. Sinless, His virtue surpassed the most virtuous who walked the earth. He labored under the Father's directive, able to proclaim, "I brought glory to you here on earth by completing the work you gave me to do" (John 17:4). He confounded the so-called wise Pharisees with His wisdom. Most of these virtues He displayed on the pathway to Golgotha. Depth of fortitude helped Him to set His face like flint toward the city of His impending death: Jerusalem. He endured the ridicule and beatings because He knew the reward that would come. He had faith to believe His Father would raise Him back to life, and, with that, welcome the world to life again.

When you read the words of Proverbs 31, I pray you'll recognize your Savior there as well as your need for Him. He reminded His disciples to wait until He was glorified because the Spirit would soon come, empowering them to live as He did on this earth.

In the second chapter of Acts, we see the fiery presence of this same Spirit, resting upon and then filling the believers. Throughout the New Testament, we see the fruits of this Spirit in action. They, too, resemble the traits of the Proverbs 31 woman. Note the overlap from Galatians 5:22–23:

- Love
- Joy
- Peace
- Patience
- Kindness
- Goodness
- Faithfulness
- Gentleness
- Self-control

If we want to leave the same kind of legacy as the Proverbs 31 woman, besides receiving the grace we need when we stumble and fall, we need the Spirit of God within us, empowering us to live in the same manner.

Stop comparing and start praying. Her traits are yours for the asking, and the ticket to receive them is simply this: acknowledging your need for the Spirit.

Truths about Fully Understood You

- You have a lifetime to create a legacy.
- Your industriousness matters.
- You always have the choice to help others.
- No matter how you may feel about your appearance, you can always be a beautiful soul.
- Relationships add texture and joy to your life.

Questions for Discussion

1. What have you felt about the Proverbs 31 woman in the past? How did this rendering of her change your opinion?
2. How does knowing she accomplished these tasks over a lifetime help you offer yourself grace?
3. Which of the Proverbs 31 woman's traits do you admire most? Which one are you currently working on with the Lord?
4. In your context, what does it look like to fear the Lord? How does that relate to charm and beauty?
5. How does our world differ from the culture of the Proverbs 31 woman? What is similar? What can you glean from her life? What can you discard?

CHAPTER NINE

Mary of Magdala, the Demonized One

To be known only as the person you were in the past keeps you tethered to your past, Mary knew. But her mind had not always been so clearheaded for such thoughts. There had been a time when seven evil spirits controlled her, forcing her to fling herself upon rocks, screech obscenities, and harass those she loved. It was almost as if she floated above herself then, looking upon a wild animal growling and striking, but she was powerless to stop its noise or bite. Helpless—that was her lot.

Until that day.

The day of sweet deliverance.

Mary had heard the rumors reach her village, Magdala, while she was still in the clutches of evil. The coastal town butted up against the Sea of Galilee, its name meaning "tower." But she did not concern herself with its welfare, content to work with textile and dyes until her fingers reddened and her eyes stung. It was on one such day she heard the name *Jesus*—a common enough name in those parts, but how her friend Sophia pronounced it stirred Mary's heart.

"There is a teacher," Sophia had told her. "His name is Jesus."

As they walked the dusty road away from their daily labor, Sophia turned to face Mary. "I know your affliction. It was the same with my Aunt Abigail—she was tormented as you are. But one day, Jesus took note of her as she writhed on the side of the road, unable to control herself."

Mary's eyes widened. "Did she hear voices?" This question she whispered, for fear her story would become even more public.

"Many," Sophia said. "But Jesus stopped, took her by the hand."

"He is a Jew?"

"Yes, a teacher, devout and kind."

"And yet he touched your aunt?"

"It seemed as natural as me touching you right now." Sophia held Mary's hands in hers, looking into her eyes.

"What happened next?"

"My aunt screamed something like, 'What have you to do with us, Jesus, the Son of God?'"

Sudden confusion and darkness fell upon Mary then. *Son of God?* The voices in her head amplified, chanting, *Crucify, crucify, crucify!* Mary backed away from Sophia. "I need to go," she said.

But Sophia touched her shoulder. "Please, just hear the end of the story. Jesus silenced the raging voices, then said, 'Come out of her!' and like that, she wept upon the ground, thanking Jesus profusely. And since that moment, she has been singing."

When was the last time I sang? Mary wondered. *Do melodies exist anymore?* She left her friend, but the story haunted her.

Four days later, whispers of Jesus coming along the shores of Galilee irresistibly wooed Mary to search for Him. She told her feet to walk, but her mind darkened with each step. *He is an imposter. He will kill you. He is your enemy,* the voices cackled. *If he touches you, you'll sink into the grave.* Still, Mary walked, muddying her feet along the shore of the great sea. She touched her disheveled hair, suddenly self-conscious about her appearance. The voices had taken all her energy, so much so that she had neglected propriety. She knew her eye sockets were darkened—the evil shouts lasted through each night, tormenting her sleep.

Do not walk another step, a voice hissed inside her.

Usually helpless to resist, a small part of will ignited when she saw the face of the man who would be her deliverer, though at the time she did not know whether He was strong enough to perform such an exorcism.

"Jesus," she whispered.

The man named Jesus should not have been able to hear her quavering voice, what with the crowds pressing against Him on the lake's shoreline, but He turned, then looked into her eyes with a glance that said, "I know you."

Jesus said something to a muscular fisherman next to Him, then walked toward her.

The nearer He came, the louder the screams erupting from within brought attention to Mary. She wanted to cast her body into the sea with a millstone, to sink into the depths, but Jesus held her gaze as she heard herself yelling blasphemies at Him. He came closer while she battled a sudden urge to grab a large stone and crush her own skull.

He reached for her hand as paralysis seized her. Convulsing, she fell to the earth. As she had so many times before, she floated above herself, helpless to stop her body from shaking, her mouth from foaming. This was a battle she would not win.

Jesus bent to the earth, dusting His knees, and held her shaking head in His calloused hands. "Mary," He said.

Still she loomed above, unable to respond.

"Be gone!" He shouted at the enemy voices inside her body.

For a terrible moment, the evil within her twisted and screamed out loud. But in the next moment, glorious light flooded into her, and she suddenly found herself in her right mind, sitting in the dust, looking into the face of Love.

"Get her something to eat and drink," the man named Jesus said to his companions. They promptly obeyed. The water upon her lips tasted like life, and the bread they offered filled her completely. Jesus lifted her to her feet and simply said, "Follow me."

Mary followed Jesus wherever He walked—as He freed others from possession, as He healed lepers, blind people, and raised those who had sunk into death. She traveled with the twelve, along with new companions like Joanna, the wife of Chuza, who had been Herod's manager, and another woman named Susanna. Together these women counted it a privilege to provide for the work Jesus did as they followed Him and learned the ways of love. She considered it her sacrificial offering, to grow this new Kingdom of the One who set people gloriously free.

Three years she gave her life, nearly forgetting her tormented existence back in Magdala. Evil seemed aloof, far away. No spirit could resist the simple words of Jesus. But as the third year waned, she noticed the demonic activity increase while Jesus grew more serious. Persecution increased. Jealousy flourished in the religious leaders, and every day, Mary swore she could hear the taunting from so long ago—not directed her way now, but His. Her prior possession, then deliverance, made her sensitive to such things. She watched in vain as Peter, the fisherman, tried to dissuade Jesus from going to Jerusalem; Jesus turned on him, called him Satan. Mary's blood cooled. Even the most stalwart disciple could experience Satan's icy grip.

At the Passover, her savior humbled Himself, becoming a lowly slave who washed His companions' feet. He encouraged them to become like Him, to serve, to take the last seat at the table, to love others unto death. And then, disturbed, He said, "One of you will betray me."

As the disciples each asked Jesus in turn, "Am I the one, Lord?" she couldn't help but wonder the same thing. Would the voices return and force her to betray Jesus? Was she the betrayer? Only one disciple notably did not ask such a heart-wrenching question—Judas Iscariot. Instead, he dipped his bread into the bowl at the precise moment Jesus did. "Hurry and do what you're going to do," Jesus told him. As Judas gathered his things, including the money purse he was always clutching, he turned and looked at Mary, his eyes yellow with evil. She shivered. She knew that gaze. She wondered if she would soon hear again the chanted words she heard so often in Magdala: *Crucify. Crucify. Crucify.*

The next day, Mary shivered in the heat of the morning looking up at the impossible scene—her savior, Jesus, agonized upon a torture device intended for the worst criminals. She knew Him to be the most innocent of innocents, yet there He was, laboring for breath, pushing up against the thick metal spikes driven through his hands and feet into the wood of the cross to catch yet another gulp of air. She felt herself trying to breathe for Him; His labor became hers. Mary heard the cackling, not merely of the religious people and the sadistic Roman guards around her—no, this was as familiar to her as her enslavement had once been. It was the howl of the enemy of humanity, screeching in laughter, enticing others to revel in the carnage in front of them. But she could not participate.

Soldiers threw lots for the clothes of the man who had fed thousands from nearly nothing. Mary's stomach soured, forcing bile up her throat. He, the one who brought true justice, suffered under the weight of an unjust trial brought by both Jews and Romans. Whipped, beaten, mocked, with flesh torn—Jesus had endured to the point of hammers falling upon the bones of His wrists and ankles. When the Romans raised the three crosses—Jesus in the center with the crime "King of the Jews" written above Him, two actual criminals flanking him—the sound of each cross thudding into the pitted earth reverberated through her. Each man gasped, then cried out.

She hated this place, Golgotha. The rock formation beneath the three crosses resembled a skull and held the stench of death. Though she knew He had the power at hand to call down a legion of angelic beings to rescue him, she also knew His resolute manner; He would endure this to the end as a faithful lamb led to slaughter.

Two other Marys stood beside her, clutching her hands and pulling in breath—dear Mary, the wife of Zebedee, the mother of James and John. Mary of Magdala wanted to embrace her, tell her all would be well, but would not that be a lie? And there was Mary, the mother of Jesus. The Lord invited John to treat her as his own mother now.

All three Marys held hands then, as Salome joined them, simply saying, "No, no, no."

The wagging of men's heads. The taunting. The evil words.

"Ha! Look at you now!" they yelled at Him.

"You said you were going to destroy the Temple and rebuild it in three days. Well then, if you are the Son of God, save yourself and come down from the cross!"

If they only knew what they were saying.

The religious elite continued their mockery. "He saved others," they scoffed, "but he can't save himself!"

"Let this Messiah, this King of Israel, come down from the cross so we can see it and believe him!"

One of the criminals hanging next to Jesus hurled abuse as well.

Mary shivered there three hours before the sun was suddenly erased from the sky at high noon. An unnatural blackness fell upon them all, and she wanted to leave this place permeated with the stench of death. Would her witnessing this hell mean she approved? Should she retreat in protest? But Mary kept looking into the eyes of Jesus, her deliverer. No, she would endure the crucifixion *with* Jesus. He needed companionship now more than at any other time in His life. He pushed himself up again, gulped in a breath, then collapsed on Himself, suffocating.

At three in the afternoon, the time of prayer, Jesus obeyed by praying, *"Eloi, Eloi, lema sabachthani?"*

If He is forsaken, she thought, *then we are all doomed to a light-less life*. The cackling around her intensified. She begged God to please protect her from the voices, as they felt near enough to taste.

A bystander filled a sponge with sour wine, holding it up to Jesus on a reed stick so He could drink. "Wait!" the people said. "Let's see whether Elijah comes to take him down!"

But Elijah did not come.

Neither did a miraculous rescue. The Miracle Man who had doled out multiplied food, healings, and deliverances so freely turned ashen. He uttered another loud cry, pushing up on the spikes, while His final breath flew to Heaven.

Immediately the group of women around her erupted in fresh sorrow, John the disciple joining their tangible grief. A Roman officer nearby, who had witnessed the entire scene, said, "This man truly was the Son of God!"

And now? This Son of God breathed no more.

What could Mary of Magdala do? Sabbath prevented any work, but the moment the sky dimmed that Saturday and sundown was assured, she joined Salome and Mary the mother of James and Joseph. Together they purchased burial spices so they could anoint the body of Jesus.

Sunday morning before daybreak, the motley group of women walked to Joseph of Arimathea's tomb. On the way, they'd talked about how they would be able to roll away the enormous stone that blocked its entrance. But as they came near, Mary noticed the stone had already been rolled aside. They entered the tomb, one after the other, ducking through the doorway hewn from rock. A young man clothed in a white robe sat on the right side. Who was this? And why did he shine?

"Don't be alarmed. You are looking for Jesus of Nazareth, who was crucified," the man in white said. "He isn't here! He is risen from the dead! Look, this is where they laid his body."

Mary took note of the empty dais, the grave clothes undisturbed except for a folded bit of linen where Jesus's head once laid.

"Now go and tell his disciples, including Peter, that Jesus is going ahead of you to Galilee," the man said. "You will see him there, just as he told you before he died."

But she could not believe such words. They made no sense to her. Alive? This was impossible. She'd heard rumors from the religious elite that at the precise moment Jesus breathed His last, the curtain separating the Holy Place from the Holy of Holies in the middle of the Temple had been rent in two, from top to bottom, as if God Himself had torn it in anguish.

She ran, breathless, to find Peter and John, recounting what she had seen. "They have taken the Lord's body out of the tomb, and we don't know where they have put him," she told them.

Both men ran to the tomb, but John arrived first. Peter entered, then John. They, too, saw the perplexing wrappings and no body. They left. Because what could they do? What did any of this mean?

The events of the week's end settled in on Mary that moment. The weight of what she had watched. The trauma of losing a dear friend. The confusion of what this all meant. Wasn't Messiah supposed to be victorious? Shouldn't they all be delivered from Rome's strangling grip? All she knew was that she felt utterly alone.

She stepped again into the tomb, but now two men in white stood there—tall, broad-shouldered, and confident. "Dear woman, why are you crying?" The men asked this simultaneously, their voices echoing off the walls of the tomb.

"Because they have taken away my Lord," she replied, "and I don't know where they have put him."

The men in white gave no response.

She turned to leave. Someone stood blocking her way. Was he the gardener sent to tend this garden tomb?

"Dear woman, why are you crying?" the gardener asked. "Who are you looking for?"

"Sir, if you have taken him away, tell me where you have put him, and I will go get him."

"Mary!" the man said. Something about his voice arrested her attention.

Jesus?

How could it be?

"Rabboni!" she cried. She fell at His feet, noticing the healed scars at His ankles, and clung to Him, weeping. How could she reconcile what she had witnessed with who stood before her now?

"Don't cling to me," Jesus said, "for I haven't yet ascended to the Father. But go find my brothers and tell them, 'I am ascending to my Father and your Father, to my God and your God.'"

Before she could ask another question—what did He mean by ascending to the Father?—He was gone. Did she dream all this?

No. Jesus was as real to her then as He had been when He delivered her of those seven terrible demons. She found her wits and ran to meet the disciples near Galilee. Breathless upon reaching them, she said, "I have seen the Lord!" Then she gave them His message.

The Biblical Narrative

It was unheard of in Roman times for women be a part of an itinerant ministry, let alone offer support for it. Women were not allowed to learn from a rabbi—in fact, there was no such thing as "coed" education in Jesus's world. Women were essentially powerless in first-century Judea, so for Jesus to include them on many levels (provision, fellowship, learning) was utterly revolutionary—and scandalous.

Couple that with a bias against those who had once been demonized, and you see just how marginalized someone like Mary of

Magdala would have been. The word for "evil" (as in the seven evil spirits who tortured young Mary) is not *kakos* (which means general evil), but *poneros*, which connotes "active evil"—the kind of evil intent on inflicting much harm.[1] Hers was not a mild inconvenience: Mary was being tortured by pure evil, no doubt hearing voices, enacting bodily harm upon herself, and never having peace. That there were seven (the number of completion) meant she was certainly traumatized beyond her own ability to save herself. Without Jesus and His deliverance, she would have stayed in this state the rest of her life.

But unlike the parable where the exorcised demon returned to its host with seven other demons more terrible than itself (see Matthew 12:45), Mary of Magdala remained demon-free throughout her life. This would mean that when she was delivered, the emptiness inside her was replaced by faith in Jesus. She was now filled with Him.

This is where the misunderstanding comes in. In the early Church, some people equated her with the sinful woman in Luke 7:36–50 who washed Jesus's feet with her hair. Because Mary of Magdala is then mentioned at the beginning of Luke 8, some lumped the two together. But there is no scriptural basis that Mary of Magdala was that woman. She is known as one of the people who provided for Jesus, as a respected citizen, according to Luke 8:1–3. Once she met Him, she lived a chaste and dedicated life.

The fact that she had been demonized did not mean she had been a prostitute. She has also been confused with Mary of Bethany, Martha's sister. But these Marys are not the same either. Perhaps the biggest reason Mary of Magdala has experienced such a character smear came from Pope Gregory the Great, who wrote, "She whom Luke calls the sinful woman, whom John calls Mary [of Bethany], we believe to be the Mary from whom seven devils were ejected according to Mark."[2]

Others have equated her with the woman caught in adultery in John 8:1–11, but again, there is no scriptural justification for such a claim.[3] That woman is not named, and the passage is not even included in some translations, as her story was added later.[4] This Mary, heralding from Magdala, was one of Jesus's most dedicated followers. At the crucifixion, she did not run (as many of the male disciples did). No, bravely she stayed, enduring the excruciating sight. (See Mark 15:40–41, Luke 23:49, Matthew 27:55–56, and John 19:25.) She helped embalm Jesus, preparing Him for burial. And, according to the Apostle John, she was the very first human being to bear witness to the resurrection (see John 20:11–18).

Mary was one of the generous givers noted in Luke 8. The Greek verb for contributing to Jesus's needs is *diakoneo*, which is cast in the imperfect tense. This means the women who provided for Jesus's ministry did this again and again. Theirs was a continued and sacrificial generosity. In fact, without support, how would Jesus have been able to spend three full years traveling, teaching, healing, and casting out demons? These women—Joanna, Susanna, Mary of Magdala, "and many others" (Luke 8:3)—sacrificed their resources so that the whole known world could experience Jesus. *Diakoneo*, besides being a continuous action, has a variety of nuances—"laboring in the dust," "running through the dust," "running errands," or "waiting on tables." Mary of Magdala, along with her compatriots, mimicked the servanthood Jesus modeled throughout His ministry. They took the lowest seat. They were happy to serve unseen. Their sacrifice made a way for all of us to hear the good news![5]

Besides Mary's long endurance throughout the ministry of Jesus, we see just how important she was during one of literature's most important scenes. Why she did not recognize the resurrected Jesus at first, or why she thought Him the gardener, cannot be fully explained. Perhaps, as the disciples encountered later, His resurrected body appeared different than before. Some scholars say she turned away quickly from him and He spoke to her back.[6] Others say tears blurred her vision.[7] Regardless, it's only when Jesus says her name that she recognizes Him. This shows the intimate connection Jesus had with Mary.

Her response? To fall down and worship Him. To cling to Him with joy.

Jesus then had a message for her—one of utmost importance. His words were those of the inaugural Gospel: that the Kingdom would be changed once He ascended to Heaven. Mary stopped her clinging, running to the disciples to deliver the first account of the resurrection: "I have seen the Lord!" From demonized to a declarer of the Good News! From unknown and unseen to the first proclaimer of the Gospel! Mary of Magdala reveals just how powerful the transformation of Jesus is in anyone's life—even those once held in the clutches of the evil one.

How Does This Apply to Misunderstood You?

Mary of Magdala was obviously misunderstood by church leaders for a millennium. Her common first name, coupled with sloppy scholarship on the part of first and second-century believers,[8] prevented many from seeing her as she really was—a formerly demonized person who was radically transformed into a faithful follower of Jesus.

Personally, I believe that during her lifetime, she was not merely misunderstood, but underestimated because of her past and her station in life. What can we do when we suffer a similar misunderstanding? When people hold us to our pasts, essentially locking us into personas we no longer resemble, we face the uncomfortable truth that some people don't like our growth or change. When I was a small child, in the throes of trauma and loneliness, I tended to be shy. I became an observer of others, often retreating to my room because the adults in my life tended to be fearsome or unreliable. But underneath all that hiding and fear lived a gregarious girl who loved people.

After I met Jesus, the real me started to emerge—with joyful vigor. I became outgoing and extroverted. I made many friends and was popular in high school. So you can imagine how maddening it became to hear a relative say things like, "Mary is such a shy person." I bristled at the words, not because being shy was wrong, but because it was no longer true of me.

Have you encountered something similar? I can imagine the whispers Mary of Magdala heard throughout her lifetime.

Isn't she the demonized one?

Who does she think she is, proclaiming the Gospel?

Why does Jesus spend time with someone like that?

Can anything good come from Magdala?

People do not welcome or like change; if you change and move forward, others may have to reevaluate their own lives. Or perhaps they're lazy and don't want to change the way they view you. It's easier to typecast you than to welcome a dynamic change.

Your best strategy when battling someone else's fixed mindset is consistency. You cannot control another's view of you, but you certainly can act admirably, according to the new you that Jesus has wrought.

A beautiful way to walk through this scripturally comes from Isaiah 43:16–21. I've divided the passage into three sections to help frame your journey.

The Past You

I am the LORD, who opened a way through the waters,
making a dry path through the sea.
I called forth the mighty army of Egypt
with all its chariots and horses.
I drew them beneath the waves, and they drowned,
  their lives snuffed out like a smoldering candlewick.
(Isaiah 43:16–17)

When you look at your past, it's important to remember how Jesus has delivered you. No doubt Mary of Magdala could recount her own enslavement to the powers of darkness, much like the Israelites could recount their time under Egyptian tyranny. When someone underestimates you or tries to keep you tied to your past, one way you remove the sting from their words is to simply agree, "Yes, that was me." And then recount the goodness of God and how He's rescued and changed you. Their misunderstanding could be an open door for sharing the Gospel!

The Present You

But forget all that—it is nothing compared to what I am going to do.
For I am about to do something new.
See, I have already begun! Do you not see it?
I will make a pathway through the wilderness.
I will create rivers in the dry wasteland. (Isaiah 43:18–19)

In the middle of this passage, we see something astonishing. While God had powerfully delivered the nation of Israel through miracles, He now tells them to forget all that. Mary of Magdala chose this route. She did not merely revel in her supernatural deliverance, but she walked away from her past toward Jesus, funding His ministry and walking alongside Him. That gave her the opportunity to see the Kingdom of God unfold through miraculous healings, powerful exorcisms, and supernatural provision (like the feeding of the five thousand and the four thousand). Jesus did far more than she imagined. And this is true of you as well. Yes, your story of deliverance matters, but it is merely the "once upon a time" to your ongoing, brand-new story. As mentioned earlier, the Apostle Paul tells us, "No eye has seen, no ear has heard, and no mind has imagined what God has prepared for those who love him" (1 Corinthians 2:9). The best is yet to come, and it constantly beckons you.

Yes, you have been healed, but you are also being healed today—and on Heaven's shores, you will be fully healed and alive.

God's heart is always for you to grow, to walk out your sanctification journey (see Philippians 2:12). Others may misunderstand you. Friends may hold you to who you were "back then." Family may try to verbally hold you captive to the past. But the truth is Jesus is always, always beckoning you forward, doing the impossible through the power of the Holy Spirit within. He is making new pathways through the wilderness. He is creating rivers in the dry wasteland.

The Future You

The wild animals in the fields will thank me,
the jackals and owls, too, for giving them water in the desert.
Yes, I will make rivers in the dry wasteland
so my chosen people can be refreshed.
I have made Israel for myself, and they will someday honor me before the whole world. (Isaiah 43:20–21)

Orienting ourselves toward the future helps us embrace resilience. The last phrase, "and they will someday honor me before the whole world," is something Mary of Magdala lived. She was delivered of demons. She walked with Jesus. She was the first to share the Gospel with a dying world!

I often share this quote from author Mark Buchanan's beautiful book *The Rest of God* when I encourage audiences to move gloriously forward. He writes of counseling a woman with a beyond-broken past. As a pastor he felt helpless to come alongside her, such was the grief she poured out. He writes,

And then God slipped me an insight, timely as manna dropped from the sky. He showed me that her past was beyond repair, at least on my watch. If there was any good thing there to salvage, I knew not how. But in the same instant God showed me she still had her future. And it was vast, unbroken, pristine, radiant.... Her past was a tragedy to lament. But her future was an epic to anticipate.[9]

Those words ring true for you as well. When others underestimate you based on the wreckage of your past, they are also missing Jesus's power to transform you. Keep moving toward that pristine future, friend. Even under the cloud of misunderstanding, your tenacity will become a testimony to the fact that God not only saves us, but that He saves us to bring us—and make us—something better.

Truths about Fully Understood You

- Being misunderstood cannot prevent you from shining your light for Jesus.
- God loves to bring freedom to you.
- No matter what your past, your present and future have a purpose, thanks to Jesus.
- Sometimes you're not called to act, but to witness what God is doing—and then share it.
- You have a testimony.

Questions for Discussion

1. Did you have any of the common misconceptions about Mary of Magdala (perhaps believing her to be a prostitute)? How did this retelling and unpacking the biblical story help you see her differently?
2. Mary was radically delivered from the dominion of darkness into the marvelous light of Jesus. How has Jesus delivered you? What did you leave behind?

3. What about Mary's story brings you hope today?
4. Who in your life best represents Mary's faithfulness to Jesus? How does that person conduct his or her life? What makes that person different?
5. Mary was generous with her resources. How can you demonstrate your stewardship this week? What has God been asking you to share? What does it mean to be generous?

CHAPTER TEN

Phoebe, the Unknown One

Phoebe felt the weight of Paul's instructions. Who was she to be entrusted with such a treasure of words? How would she traverse the unknown world between Cenchrea and Rome as a woman? Paul's commendation was clear in the letter; this was true. But would she be received? And more importantly, had she spent enough time with the text and its author to be able to adequately translate its essence to her audience?

As a deaconess, she knew responsibility. It kept her up at night, pushed her to her knees, held her close to Jesus, her savior and friend. In the light of day, the mood lightened somewhat—the sun had a way of reminding her of new mercies every morning. In the morning courtyard, Paul stood, then paced. "This is our last moment together," he said.

She sensed his reticence. Phoebe readjusted her *palla*, then sheltered her eyes with her right hand. The brightness belied the seriousness of their conversation. She sat on the stone bench opposite Paul's pacing. "Yes, it is," she finally said.

"I trust you." His words felt like a proclamation, no indictment hidden within.

She let out a breath, tracing her hands over the worn stone. "I will not let you down," she heard herself say. But there was so much that could take place between Paul's writing the letter to the believers in Rome and the actual journey she would take across the known world to deliver it. A long walk. Several ships' journeys. And more walking. And then, what of the hidden church? In the foreign streets of Rome, would she be able to find Priscilla and Aquila? Was the map she carried correct?

"Phoebe," Paul said. "You know my heart. You have labored with me over the ink, the intentions. You have lived its message. Surely God in Heaven will go before you, beside you. He has already redeemed you from so much. Is He not trustworthy now?"

"Aye." She nodded. She remembered the moment she'd first heard the Good News, how before that she had chased satisfaction in serving Apollo, but ultimately found life utterly empty. It was as if God knew her breaking point, and, at precisely that moment of near-suicide, provided a believer to share about Jesus Christ—His perfect life, horrific death on behalf of pagan sinners like herself, and beautiful resurrection. The story captured her, then captivated her heart. The moment she prayed alongside her new companion, she felt the heavens open before her. She spoke another language as joy engulfed her. She had never been the same since, and though her family persecuted what they called her "crazy foolishness," she grew in her new faith like a field of poppies in sunshine.

Paul continued his pacing as the sun grew hot in the sky, warming the courtyard. "You must tell them about the world, how the whole earth has no excuse," he said.

"Of course. You have written about that in the beginning of the letter." She looked at the scroll Paul held as he paced, then mustered up her memory. If the scroll ever fell into maleficent hands, or if she dropped it by accident into the mighty Mediterranean Sea, her mind would hold it captive still. "Yes, they knew God, but they wouldn't worship him as God or even give him thanks. And they began to think up foolish ideas of what God was like. As a result, their minds became dark and confused. Claiming to be wise, they instead—"

"—became utter fools," Paul finished her sentence. "And instead of worshiping the glorious, ever-living God, they worshiped idols made to look like mere people and birds and animals and reptiles." With this, he sat nearby at the end of the long stone bench. He set the scroll between them. "You have learned it well."

"More than that," Phoebe said, "I want to live it well. I want to be an example of goodness, strength, and the power of the Gospel."

Paul looked at her with marine-blue eyes, then nodded. "You are such a woman—a woman after God's own heart. It is why I have chosen you for such a task."

"It is a great task." She touched the scroll between them. "I will faithfully carry out your intentions," she said.

"Phoebe, my sister, you are a servant, a helper of many. It is why I chose you."

She could feel the blush of her cheek. But even more than Paul's kind words, she felt the favor of God to entrust her with such a task—to carry this masterpiece to hungry believers.

Several members of the church of Cenchrea gathered in the court-yard then, laying hands upon her and praying fervently for her voyage. When the last *amen* reverberated off the stone, she looked up, eyes wet, and thanked everyone.

Paul took her hand in his, gave her one final gaze, and said, "God-speed, Phoebe of Cenchrea."

Her sandals rubbed her feet raw, and blisters birthed blisters as her journey took her to the coast. There at the port, she boarded a semi-seaworthy vessel, hoping it would hold its own against the fickle waters whose weather shifted like a serpent. She battled both

seasickness and loneliness. The pouch into which she had carefully
tucked the scroll she guarded with her life, which meant nighttime
became sleepless. By the time she reached her first destination to board
another vessel that would take her nearer to Rome, she worried she
would not have the stamina to endure the next leg. But she persisted.
And every moment the Almighty would allow, she would share the
Good News of Jesus Christ with the pagan seafarers. Most scoffed,
but one, Cassius, listened with earnest.

As the welcomed sun calmed the sea beneath the vessel, Cassius
plied her with questions. "How can you know God made the sea?" he
asked as he sanded the weather-worn deck.

"He is not the God of the sea only," she said, "but of sky and earth
and people. While many have fragmented God into little deities over
small estates, our God is the creator of all things, everything you see."
She pointed to the sky.

"How does this correlate to Jesus?" he asked.

"He is God's Son, the One sent to live a perfect life so we could
experience forgiveness."

"This all seems like superstition." He continued sanding.

Phoebe remembered the words in her carefully guarded scroll.
"We are made right with God by placing our faith in Jesus Christ. And
this is true for everyone who believes, no matter who we are," she said.

"I doubt that kind of powerful God would want me to follow
Him. You do not know what I have done." Cassius cleared his throat.

Phoebe shaded her eyes. "You are not alone in this thought," she
said. "For everyone has sinned; we all fall short of God's glorious
standard. Yet God, in His grace, freely makes us right in his sight. He
did this through Christ Jesus when He freed us from the penalty for
our sins."

Cassius continued to question, while Phoebe quoted the scroll,
revealing its mystery. And as she did, she prayed that God would open
the heart of the man with the calloused hands. When she disembarked,

she prayed God would allow the seed she had planted to grow in his heart. "Cassius," she said as she disembarked, "you are loved."

"Thank you," he said. "I will not soon forget your words."

Phoebe prayed her feet would callous over quickly for the long walk between the port and the great, terrible city of Rome. She knew to walk eastward up the hill until she hit the famed Appian Way, the Roman road that would lead her northward, eventually leading her into the heart of the city. After a long day's trek under an unrelenting sun, feet nearly bleeding, she found an inn for the evening. Locked behind the bedroom door, she could finally collapse into sleep—and did so, forsaking dinner. Her slumber ended with the dawn, and the march of broken feet commenced again.

After three days spent this way, Rome loomed before her, a city shining in its splendor—everything her fellow church members had said it would be. Phoebe pulled out the map from beneath her long cloak and studied its turns. One right. Two lefts. A hairpin turn. Then several paces until she came to a dead end where she was to knock upon the tentmakers' door.

As instructed by Paul, she knocked. Three times.

A small window at the top of the heavy door opened, revealing a woman's face. "Yes?"

Phoebe pulled in a breath. "I am Phoebe of Cenchrea. I have a letter from the Apostle Paul. Is this the home of Priscilla and Aquila?"

The little window shut abruptly. For a long moment, Phoebe stood there, wondering if she had miscounted her turns or steps. It was entirely possible in this catty-cornered city full of oddly angled streets. But then the larger door creaked open on metal hinges. The woman stood before her now with outstretched arms.

"I am Priscilla!" she said, then embraced Phoebe, kissing each cheek.

Phoebe let out the breath she felt she'd been holding her entire trip. *I am home,* she thought.

Priscilla ushered Phoebe into the rock-hewn home. "This is our business, residence, and church," she explained. "Aquila and I take in believers who work alongside us. We shelter those suffering persecution. And we have to be cautious about who we allow into this compound. But you?" She smiled. "Just hearing the apostle's name brought me such joy. It has been a long time since we have seen him. How is he, pray tell?" She ushered Phoebe into the central courtyard and spread a blanket before her. "Before you answer, recline, and let us refresh you from your hard journey."

Phoebe sat upon the beautiful tapestry, welcoming a cup of cold water and a basket full of freshly baked flatbread. "Thank you," she said.

"And Paul? How is he?" A man suddenly stood above her, bearded and joyful. "I am sorry. I have forgotten my manners." He sat across from Phoebe. "I am Aquila. I am anxious to hear from you."

"Let's wait until she's eaten, dear Aquila. I know you are excited, but she must be tired," Priscilla said.

So they broke bread together. When they finished the meal, Phoebe retrieved the scroll from her pack. She carefully unrolled it to the end, then read, "I commend to you our sister Phoebe, who is a deacon in the church in Cenchrea. Welcome her in the Lord as one who is worthy of honor among God's people." She felt herself blush, even now. "Help her in whatever she needs, for she has been helpful to many, and especially to me."

"We certainly greet you, dear sister," Aquila said.

Phoebe continued, "Give my greetings to Priscilla and Aquila, my coworkers in the ministry of Christ Jesus. In fact, they once risked their lives for me. I am thankful for them, and so are all the Gentile churches. Also give my greetings to the church that meets in their home."

A roar of laughter and applause echoed off the stone walls. "Our friend Paul has not forgotten us," Aquila said.

A day later, the small but faithful congregation gathered before Phoebe. Though she had memorized Paul's letter to this church, she knew that performing it precisely as Paul had—with his inflections and emphases—would be far easier with the text before her. And so she began, "This letter is from Paul, a slave of Christ Jesus, chosen by God to be an apostle and sent out to preach His Good News."

The Biblical Narrative

I am fortunate enough to have written a novel about Phoebe and her likely journey to Rome.[1] This allowed me extensive time to research her relatively unknown and obscure life. Truly, her role in the early Church was profound. Most scholars agree that, if a letter were to be transported, the person conveying it would receive a commendation, usually at the letter's end. We read Paul's words about her above in the narrative (from Romans 16:1–2).

The name *Phoebe* means "bright and radiant," "pure," or "radiant as the moon."[2] Hers is a Gentile name, closely resembling "Phoibe," the name of a pagan goddess. Some scholars connect the name to a feminine form of Apollo, the god whose name means "bright one."[3] It was common for believers to keep their pagan names, as they no longer held any power or meaning after turning to Christ. In a way, it became part of one's testimony: *I was once a pagan (notice my name!), but now I am completely new.*[4]

Phoebe came from Cenchrea, a thriving seaport about eight miles east of Corinth on the Gulf of Saronicus.[5] The church she attended there would certainly stand out amid the city's many pagan altars and shrines. Nearby Corinth was the place where Paul shaved his head to fulfill a vow during his third missionary journey. This is most likely where and when the two first met.

The word *commend* here is *sunistao*, literally meaning "to set together" or "to present."[6] Digging a little deeper, we find the word means "to vouch for" or "recommend as worthy of confidence or notice."[7] These are no small words from the apostle to Aquila and Priscilla, the recipients of the letter to the Roman church. The messenger's identity and presence was essential to reassure believers that a letter was truly penned by Paul (or any of the other disciples who wrote to the early Church). This was Phoebe's letter of introduction, Paul's way of saying, "She is worthy of carrying these words, and I have put my full confidence in her." Paul's commendation could also secure housing and safe passage for Phoebe as she traveled by land and boat to Rome.

Paul describes Phoebe in three ways: "sister," "deacon," and "helpful to many."

Phoebe is first a sister—not by birth, but through new birth. She is fully accepted in the family of God, redeemed and set free.

She is a deaconess (*diakonos*), or servant, in her local congregation—one entrusted to help others. This same word is used in Romans 13:4 to refer to the government. This role, therefore, held a level of authority. In Acts 6, we read about the first appointment of deacons, people tasked with taking care of the growing needs of widows and orphans in the burgeoning congregations. "Select seven men who are well respected and are full of the Spirit and wisdom. We will give them this responsibility" (Acts 6:3). It's important to note that Stephen—the Church's first martyr and a brilliant orator with a heart for Christ—was one of the seven selected. Appointing deacons meant that "God's message continued to spread" (Acts 6:7). Deacons were not merely grunts who did unseen work; they were the important backbone of church growth and spreading salvation.

Paul reminds the embryonic Church what type of believers they should choose as deacons:

> In the same way, deacons must be well respected and have integrity. They must not be heavy drinkers or dishonest

with money. They must be committed to the mystery of the faith now revealed and must live with a clear conscience. Before they are appointed as deacons, let them be closely examined. If they pass the test, then let them serve as deacons. (1 Timothy 3:8–10)

Superimpose these rigorous standards over Phoebe, and you find a woman full of trustworthiness, integrity, and temperance, typifying good stewardship and generosity. She loves the Gospel, and she lives in such a way that she passes all the tests set before her.

The word Paul uses for "helper to many" here is *prostasis*, meaning "one who stands over."[8] The term is commonly used for wealthy patrons. In Greek, the word is used to describe a trainer of Olympic athletes, an ancient coach. The Amplified Bible describes Phoebe, in Paul's words, as "a helper of many including myself, shielding us from suffering." There's authority in the way Phoebe serves; she has a protective nature that shields others from harm. She is not passive, but quite proactive—a champion of others. Because Paul chooses her to transport the letter (coupled with the common use of *prostasis*), there is a strong indication that Phoebe was also a person of means, someone who provided for the local ministry through her resources.

So when Paul commends her to the believers in Rome, the connotation is clear. Phoebe is an important member of her local church. She should be completely welcomed and honored because of her service. The Roman believers are to *prosdechomai* her—to earnestly accept her with favor. When Paul tells them to welcome her in a manner worthy of honor, he means to give weight to her office. Another way of saying this is that "Their welcome [of Paul's emissary] should weigh as much as the position [that person holds] in the family of God."[9] They should help her in practical ways, as well; the Greek term is *pragma*, from which we get our word *pragmatic*.

Those who delivered ancient letters were not merely postal workers. They were also tasked with knowing the emphasis of each phrase, to be so well acquainted with the writer's phraseology that they could successfully "perform" the letter, acting it out using the author's voice inflections. This was not a monotone reading, but a powerful elocution. Phoebe would have to have been with Paul as he wrote the letter, or at least spent a great deal of time with him to best understand its heart as well as its contents. Most likely she memorized the letter, as many did in her profoundly oral culture. She also would have had to know how Paul sounded as he read it, then read it to her listeners the same way.

How Does This Apply to Misunderstood You?

Phoebe was faithful without fanfare. She quietly served and ful-filled her mission, yet with bravery, planning and securing her journey over land and sea from Cenchrea to Rome—no doubt a perilous journey. She is mentioned nowhere else in Scripture, but can you imagine our world without the book of Romans in it? She was an emissary of extreme importance, yet so few realize the profound role she played.

Perhaps the deepest misunderstanding believers can face is that of insignificance. In a world of splash and instant fame, we forget the upside-down nature of the Kingdom, where the last are first and the first are last. In order to thrive in today's popularity-obsessed culture, we must reorient our hearts toward the correct kingdom.

In God's Kingdom, unknown people like Phoebe are tasked with important work. In the world, only the superstars are counted as significant. When our significance is only tied to how well-known we are, we can crumble when that recognition isn't there. Real work is feet to the ground fueled by a servant's heart. We find our significance not by preening for the crowd, but by seeking to please an audience of

One. Like John the Baptist, we cry, "He [Jesus] must become greater and greater, and I must become less and less" (John 3:30).

Jesus heralds the small, but we elevate the large. Yet when you read the parables of Christ, you may be struck by their heroes. A small, insignificant mustard seed becomes a big tree. An overlooked widow finds justice. A little yeast leavens the entire lump of dough. The pearl is small, but of inestimable value. The youngest son is feted by his father. The outcast Samaritan saves the day, to the shame of the religious elite who ignored a broken, bleeding man. A single sheep merits leaving ninety-nine behind. Jesus reminds us of the power of small when He says, "If you are faithful in little things, you will be faithful in large ones. But if you are dishonest in little things, you won't be honest with greater responsibilities" (Luke 16:10).

Friends, coworkers, church members, or your family of origin may misunderstand your significance, but in the Kingdom of God, all followers of Christ are important. The smallest ministry, when fueled by the Spirit of God, is amplified. Jesus reminds us what true ministry is. It is not necessarily flashy or powerful, but humble and unseen. "And if you give even a cup of cold water to one of the least of my followers, you will surely be rewarded," He reminds us in Matthew 10:42.

In order to execute what may seem like a pointless or unseen assignment, we must cultivate an inner fortitude, finding joy in doing what is right despite the temporal reward or lack thereof. When I've felt the sting of "insignificant" ministry, I've reminded myself that this world is not all there is. "Give your gifts in private," Jesus reminds us, "and your Father, who sees everything, will reward you" (Matthew 6:4). He sees your toil. He gives weighty significance to your faithful, quiet work.

When you feel insignificant, remind yourself of these powerful affirmations rooted in Scripture:

- Someday I will see Jesus, and all this obscure toiling will make sense. (2 Corinthians 5:8, Titus 2:13)

- I will obtain a non-perishable inheritance that won't fade. (1 Peter 1:4)
- When I feel insignificant, I will set my mind on eternity. (Colossians 3:2)
- I will be patient for the increase God will give me. (James 5:7)
- When I am discouraged, I will fix my eyes on what is unseen. (2 Corinthians 4:8)
- In a battle, I will ask God to open my eyes to what is really happening around me. (2 Kings 6)
- My integrity is more important than my status. (2 Peter 3:11–14)
- I may not get my reward now, but I wait for my eternal reward with expectation. (Hebrews 11:26)
- When I feel stressed and overwhelmed, I will view my circumstances as the momentary afflictions they are. (2 Corinthians 4:16–18)
- I will persevere, knowing many before me endured well. (Hebrews 11:13–16)
- When I despair and fear, I will remind myself of how God will make all things new and beautiful in Heaven. (Isaiah 25:6–8)
- When overlooked, I will remember that my present sufferings are nothing in comparison with the glory that will come my way. (Romans 8:18)
- When I am unfulfilled, I will remind myself of the fulfillment that awaits me. (Luke 6:20–23)
- When I face misunderstanding, I will focus on the moment I finally see the face of Jesus. (Revelation 22:3–4)
- When I'm walking through a long trial, I will remind myself of the brevity of this life. (James 4:13–14)

- When others flaunt their treasures and stature, I will focus on the kind of treasure that lasts for eternity. (Matthew 6:19–24)
- When I am unrewarded, I'll focus on eternal rewards. (2 Corinthians 5:9–10, 1 Corinthians 4:5, Matthew 25:14–30)

Much of our lives are lived unseen by people. But as the Prophet Zechariah warns, we must "not despise these small beginnings, for the Lord rejoices to see the work begin" (Zechariah 4:10). If we give into the lie that insignificance will always be our lot, we won't take the next necessary step. We must rest in knowing God understands us, and when He calls us to a task, He can see the end product. If we let the opinions of others sideline us, we won't exercise our faith.

Phoebe may be an unknown heroine of the New Testament, but she was well known by her God. She most likely kept a close connection with her Savior, hearing His voice and obeying His call. She quietly and faithfully served her church in Cenchrea, no doubt for several years, before the great task of carrying Paul's letter came to her. That she obeyed should encourage you. When danger loomed before her, she defied fear and stepped out into the unknown, living by faith—not in others and their fickle opinions, but in the God who had always been faithful to her.

The extent to which you endure and thrive when others deny your significance is the degree to which you've cultivated a deep, abiding relationship with the One who created you. In that place, the winds and seas of others' misunderstandings may batter against you, but your feet will be standing upon the firm foundation of Jesus Christ. Be someone who faithfully follows His teachings. He says they have built "a house on solid rock. Though the rain comes in torrents and the floodwaters rise and the winds beat against that house, it won't collapse because it is built on bedrock" (Matthew 7:24b–25). Don't stand on the shifting foundation of other people's opinions about what you should do with your life. Jesus warns, "But anyone who hears my teaching and doesn't obey it is foolish, like a person who builds a house on sand. When the rains and floods come and the winds beat against that house, it will collapse with a mighty crash" (Matthew 7:26–27).

Psalm 40 has comforted me for many years, echoing my testimony of God's ability to ground a life:

> I waited patiently for the LORD to help me,
> and he turned to me and heard my cry.
> He lifted me out of the pit of despair,
> out of the mud and the mire.
> He set my feet on solid ground
> and steadied me as I walked along. (Psalm 40:1–2)

That's certainly what He did with the once-pagan Phoebe. He rescued her. She remained faithful in obscurity. And then God entrusted her with a weighty task. All that to say: don't give up, friend. Keep taking the next step. Trust that your unseen work matters for eternity. There is great reward for quiet faithfulness. Your audience, the Creator of the Universe, understands you implicitly, and He will reward your work.

Every time you read the book of Romans, remind yourself that God uses seemingly insignificant people to do extraordinary work. This is how our God operates. He searches for faithful hearts, and then supports them with His strength. "The eyes of the LORD search the whole earth in order to strengthen those whose hearts are fully committed to him" (2 Chronicles 16:9). May you be like Phoebe, fully committed and empowered for Kingdom adventures!

Truths about Fully Understood You

- God has specifically gifted you for the tasks He entrusts to you.
- The presence of God in difficult journeys is available to you.
- Even when you feel alone, you never are.
- Your obedience to the call of God is beautiful.
- God takes notice of you, your dreams, and your abilities.

Questions for Discussion

1. Was there anything about Phoebe's story that surprised you? Knowing that it was common practice for a courier of a letter to "perform" it with the intention and inflection of the author, how does that change your view of Phoebe?

2. When was the last time God asked you to take a difficult journey? What happened? How was God faithful to you?

3. What would the Bible be like without the book of Romans? What would we be missing if no one had delivered it to Rome?

4. Which of Phoebe's qualities would you like to emulate? Why?

5. Most likely Phoebe had been a pagan prior to meeting Christ. Her new life differed from her past life. How has Christ transformed your life?

Misunderstood No More

Thank you for journeying through the Scriptures to meet ten courageous yet misunderstood women. I pray you now more clearly understand Eve, Hagar, Leah, Rahab, Naomi, Bathsheba, Tamar, the Proverbs 31 woman, Mary of Magdala, and Phoebe. I hope their courageous journeys inform the way you live in this world full of misunderstanding.

There is solace in knowing that this world is fading, and all that it deems valuable will ebb away. 1 John 2:15–17 puts it succinctly:

> Do not love this world nor the things it offers you, for when you love the world, you do not have the love of the Father in you. For the world offers only a craving for physical pleasure, a craving for everything we see, and pride in our achievements and possessions. These are not from the Father, but are from this world. And this world is fading away, along with everything that people crave. But anyone who does what pleases God will live forever.

I pray you close this book with that kind of restorative perspective—a renewed vision for what God values versus the fickle opinions of others. Even our craving for recognition and complete understanding will fade. When you finish life's race, all will be well. Tears will be wiped away. Broken relationships will be a thing of the past. What will remain is what we did on this earth to please our God.

Don't allow the narrow boxes people have crammed you into inform your behavior. Will people misunderstand you? Yes. Will you misunderstand the ones you love? Yes. But God is the one who sees, hears, and perfectly understands you. He is the one who will defend you. Job poignantly wrote, "You must defend my innocence, O God, since no one else will stand up for me" (Job 17:3). Even if no one else understands you for the rest of your life, your Savior will perfectly understand everything you're walking through. The Lord will be your sweet vindication. Rest in the promises of Isaiah 54:16–17:

> I have created the blacksmith
> who fans the coals beneath the forge
> and makes the weapons of destruction.
> And I have created the armies that destroy.
> But in that coming day
> no weapon turned against you will succeed.
> You will silence every voice raised up to accuse you.
> These benefits are enjoyed by the servants of the LORD;
> their vindication will come from me.
> I, the LORD, have spoken!

His is the final word, the only Word that carries eternal weight. Rest there, misunderstood friend.

Acknowledgements

I'm so grateful for folks at Salem Books who have championed, honed, and strengthened this manuscript. I'm also indebted to Cynthia Ruchti, agent extraordinaire, who encouraged me through the writing of this book.

I'm grateful to the Writing Prayer Circle who have prayed for me over a decade—each book! Gratitude goes to Kathi, Sandi, Holly, Renee, Caroline, Cheramy, Jeanne, D'Ann, Darren, Dorian, Erin, Helen, Katy G., Katy R., Anita, Diane, Cyndi, Leslie, Liz, Rebecca, Sarah, Tim, Tina, Nicole, Tosca, TJ, Patrick, Jody, Susan, Becky, Dena, Carol, Susie, Christy, Alice, Randy, Paul, Jan, Thomas, Judy, Aldyth, Sue, Brandilyn, Lisa, Richard, Michele, Yanci, Cristin, Roy, Michelle, Ocieanna, Denise, Heidi, Kristin, Sarah, Phyllis, Emilie, Lea Ann, Boz, Patricia, Anna, Kendra, Gina, Ralph, Sophie, Anna, Jodie, Hope, Ellen, Lacy, Tracy, Susie May, Becky, Paula, John, Julie, Dusty, Tabea, Jessica, Cheri, Shelley, Elaine, Ally, and Amy. Thank you for your faithful prayers and your heart for this book.

For the theological acumen of my husband Patrick, I am so grateful.

And to Jesus, the one who understands being misunderstood far more than any other person, thank you for living on this earth, empathizing with my weaknesses, and setting me aright. I love that you both see and hear us.

Notes

Chapter One: Eve, the Blamed One

1. Joey Cochran, "When Adam Named Eve," CBMW.org, November 13, 2013, https://cbmw.org/2013/11/13/when-adam-named-eve/.
2. Oswald Chambers, "One of God's Great Don'ts," *My Utmost for His Highest*, https://utmost.org/classic/one-of-god%E2%80%99s-great-don%E2%80%99ts-classic.

Chapter Four: Rahab, the Prostituted One

1. Robin Ngo, "Rahab the Harlot?" Biblical Archaeology Society, September 23, 2013, https://www.biblicalarchaeology.org/daily/people-cultures-in-the-bible/people-in-the-bible/rahab-the-harlot/.
2. Ibid.

Chapter Six: Bathsheba, the Harmed One

1. Tirzah Meacham, "Female Purity (Niddah)," Jewish Women's Archive, https://jwa.org/encyclopedia/article/female-purity-niddah.
2. Blue Letter Bible, *lāqah*, https://www.blueletterbible.org/lang/lexicon/lexicon.cfm?t=kjv&strongs=h3947.
3. "David's Rape of Bathsheba and Murder of Uriah (2 Samuel 11-12)," Theology of Work, https://www.theologyofwork.org/old-testament/samuel-kings-chronicles-and-work/the-golden-age-of-the-monarchy-2-samuel-1-24-1-kings-1-11-1-chronicles-21-2/davids-successes-and-failures-as-king-2-samuel-1-24/davids-rape-of-bathsheba-and-murder-of-uriah-2-samuel-11-12.
4. *Nacham* definition, Bible Hub, https://biblehub.com/hebrew/5162.htm.

Chapter Seven: Tamar, the Violated One

1. "What Did It Mean to Tear One's Clothes in the Bible?" Got Questions, https://www.gotquestions.org/tear-clothes-Bible.html.

2. "KJV Dictionary Definition: desolate," AV1611, https://av1611.com /kjbp/kjv-dictionary/desolate.html.
3. Oswald Chambers, *My Utmost for His Highest* (Grand Rapids, MI: Our Daily Bread Publishing, Classic Edition 2017), 49.
4. The author has painted many of these statements and created cards with these promises in her Etsy shop. You can find them here: etsy.com/shop/marydemuthart.

Chapter Eight: The Proverbs 31 Woman, the Perfect One

1. For a delineation of the different people King Lemuel could be, see Dr. Claude Mariottini—Professor of Old Testament, "Who Was King Lemuel?" May 18, 2009, https://claudemariottini.com/2009/05/18/ who-was-king-lemuel/.
2. See an exploration of that idea here: Rachel Darnell, "The Proverbs 31 Husband," Fathom, May 1, 2018, https://www.fathommag.com/stories/ the-proverbs-31-husband.
3. Ibid.
4. David Guzik, "Proverbs 31—The Wisdom of King Lemuel," Enduring Word Bible Commentary, https://enduringword.com/bible -commentary/proverbs-31.
5. Ibid.
6. See Proverbs 31:21, Pulpit Commentary, Bible Hub, https://biblehub. com/commentaries/pulpit/proverbs/31.htm.
7. See note on Phoenician purple dye, "Phoenician Trade, Seafaring, Purple Dye and Mining," Facts and Details, https://factsanddetails .com/world/cat56/sub371/item1982.html.

Chapter Nine: Mary of Magdala, the Demonized One

1. "Luke 8 Commentary," Precept Austin, updated April 29, 2021, https:// www.preceptaustin.org/luke-8-commentary.
2. Sarah Pruitt, "How Early Church Leaders Downplayed Mary Magdalen's Influence by Calling Her a Whore," History.com, updated April 2, 2021, https://www.history.com/news/mary-magdalene-jesus -wife-prostitute-saint.
3. See James Carroll, "Who Was Mary Magdalene?" *Smithsonian Magazine*, June 2006, https://www.smithsonianmag.com/history/who -was-mary-magdalene-119565482/.

4. See Chris Keith, "Manuscript History and John 8:1-8:11," Bible Odyssey, https://www.bibleodyssey.org/en/passages/related-articles/Manuscript-History-and-John.
5. "Luke 8 Commentary," Precept Austin, updated April 29, 2021, https://www.preceptaustin.org/luke-8-commentary.
6. See Jimmy Wallace, "Why Didn't Mary Recognize the Resurrected Jesus," Cold-Case Christianity, January 12, 2015, https://coldcasechristianity.com/writings/why-didnt-mary-recognize-the-resurrected-jesus/.
7. See Paul Brown, "Why Are You Crying?" Western North Carolina Conference, United Methodist Church, April 3, 2018, https://www.wnccumc.org/blogdetail/why-are-you-crying-11128107.
8. Again, see Carroll, "Who Was Mary Magdalene?" for how the early church fathers misinterpreted Mary of Magdala.
9. Mark Buchanan, *The Rest of God* (Nashville, TN: Thomas Nelson Publishers, 2007), 209–10.

Chapter Ten: Phoebe, the Unknown One

1. You can learn more about *A Perilous Journey* at https://www.shopguideposts.org/fiction/ordinary-women-of-the-bible-book-6-perilous-journey.html.
2. See "Lockyer's All the Women of the Bible—Phebe, Phoebe," Bible Gateway, https://www.biblegateway.com/resources/all-women-bible/Phebe-Phoebe.
3. "Romans 16:1–4 Commentary," Precept Austin, updated June 29, 2020, https://www.preceptaustin.org/romans_16_word_studies.
4. Ibid.
5. "Cenchrea—a port of Corinth," HolyLandPhotos Blog, May 27, 2021, https://holylandphotos.wordpress.com/2021/05/27/cenchrea-a-port-of-corinth/.
6. "Romans 16:1–4 Commentary."
7. Ibid.
8. Ibid.
9. Ibid.